# Make
# It Fly!

# Make It Fly!

## The step-by-step guide to make ANY idea, project or goal take off

Brigitte Cobb

**PEARSON**

Harlow, England • London • New York • Boston • San Francisco • Toronto • Sydney
Auckland • Singapore • Hong Kong • Tokyo • Seoul • Taipei • New Delhi
Cape Town • São Paulo • Mexico City • Madrid • Amsterdam • Munich • Paris • Milan

**Pearson Education Limited**

Edinburgh Gate
Harlow CM20 2JE
United Kingdom
Tel: +44 (0)1279 623623
Web: www.pearson.com/uk

**First edition published** 2013 (print and electronic)

© Brigitte Cobb 2013 (print and electronic)

The right of Brigitte Cobb to be identified as author of this work has been asserted by her in accordance with the Copyright, Designs and Patents Act 1988.

Pearson Education is not responsible for the content of third-party internet sites.

ISBN: 978-0-273-78539-2 (print)
         978-0-273-79453-0 (PDF)
         978-0-273-79454-7 (ePub)

*British Library Cataloguing-in-Publication Data*
A catalogue record for the print edition is available from the British Library

*Library of Congress Cataloging-in-Publication Data*
Cobb, Brigitte.
  Make it fly! : the step-by-step guide to make ANY idea, project or goal take off / Brigitte Cobb. -- First edition.
      pages cm
  Includes bibliographical references and index.
  ISBN 978-0-273-78539-2 (pbk. : alk. paper)
  1. Goal (Psychology) 2. Planning. 3. Change (Psychology) 4. Organizational change. I. Title.
  BF505.G6C63 2013
  158--dc23
                                      2013017462

10 9 8 7 6 5 4 3 2 1
17 16 15 14 13

Cover design by Dan Mogford

Print edition typeset in 9.5/13pt Mundo Sans Std by 3
Print edition printed and bound in Great Britain by Henry Ling, at the Dorset Press, Dorchester, Dorset.

NOTE THAT ANY PAGE CROSS REFERENCES REFER TO THE PRINT EDITION

To my husband John, for believing in me and for always being supportive of my needs. The journey would not be the same without you.

To my children, Charlotte, Antony and George, may this book prove that you can have whatever you set your mind to.

To my mum, for encouraging me to keep an open mind, and to my dad, for pushing me to get out there and fly on my own.

# CONTENTS

# ABOUT THE AUTHOR

I love change and making things happen. As a result, I've spent the past 15 years working with business clients to transform their organisations as well as lecturing on change management at Birkbeck College (University of London) and Kingston University. I hold qualifications in project, programme and organisational change management.

My passion for change and making things happen doesn't stop at business. I've been seriously interested in personal development since I read my first book on positive thinking 20 years ago and realised I had a choice in what happened to me. This passion has led to qualifications in NLP and coaching, to an extensive book collection, many seminars and some truly interesting experiences.

In recent years, I've had a vision of combining my business and personal development experience to build an execution framework for personal projects and to help people who have great ideas but are unclear how to make them happen. In my view, having ideas isn't the issue, 'making them happen' is.

My style is clear and practical. I have a reputation for being able to translate thoughts and theory into action, and for believing that we can all have and be much more than we think.

# CONNECT WITH BRIGITTE

Discover the companion website and blog at

www.brigittecobb.com

Twitter: **http://twitter.com/MakeItFly-DoIt**

Facebook: **http://facebook.com/MakeItFlyTheBook**

LinkedIn: **http://linkedin.com/in/brigittecobb**

# INTRODUCTION

## Making things happen is really very simple, if you know how and you're willing to put some effort in

What if I told you that there is a recipe for making things happen? A list of steps you can follow to get what you want in life. Steps that will show you where to start, where to go next and how to keep going. A method you can apply to anything you want, big or small, whether you wish to become healthier, start your own business or plan the wedding of the century. Wouldn't that be great?

During my research for this book, I've asked around and found that many of us have personal projects or ambitions but that very few actually know how to make them real. When I've asked people why, I've been told:

"I'm not sure where to start."

"I'm not sure if this is a good idea."

"I don't have enough time/money/skills [insert excuse] to do this."

I have spent my life making things happen at home and at work. It's a passion, I get a kick out of it and I always have a project on the go. I've changed careers several times, started more than one business, lost weight twice after my kids were born, renovated and moved house, emigrated, organised countless events including weddings and birthday parties, and written a book. I've also helped countless clients achieve their visions. Through all these experiences, successes and mistakes included, I've learnt how to turn my aspirations and those of others into reality. I know where to start, how to figure out where to go next and how to tell whether something is a good idea. I also know how to deal with challenges and work through excuses. And each time I achieve something new, I pretty much follow the same path. So, when I hear someone say "I don't know where to start", I get a very strong urge to show them.

Years ago I took everything I learnt about making stuff happen and organised it into a logical model, which I initially used at work. I didn't have plans to publicise the model; I just wanted a method I could follow when helping people make the changes they were after. Because I used the method for real and over a fairly long period of time, I refined it. The interesting thing I noticed is that the people around me were quite keen to stick to one discipline, whilst I enjoyed mixing in the method anything I found that worked, whether the technique came from the business world or personal development. As I became better and better at seeing mine and other people's wishes become real, I got even more fascinated by the process and any book or article that dealt with change, and if I found something in there I thought was interesting, I'd try it and incorporate it if useful.

I believe that there are only three things that stand between you and what you want: you need to have a good idea of what that is, you need to know how to go about getting it, and you need to deal with the stuff that scares you, slows you down or limits you. Let me tell you a secret: people who make things happen are not lucky. I've heard the phrase "she's landed on her feet again" many times when I've achieved something. It's always made me smile because of course it looks like this to an outsider. They weren't there when I was struggling with the challenges. All they see is the finished product, the achievement.

But if you ask the people close to me, they tell a different story. They will say that I don't just land on my feet. Every time I've achieved something, I knew what I wanted, I worked through my fears and I took lots of actions. They'll tell you that like everyone else I have days when I'm frustrated and I want to give up. That the first thing I try doesn't always work. That there are often people trying to put me off my goals. My husband recently told me that for a good year, when I would talk about this book to people, they would smile at me but their eyes would say "yeah, yeah, yeah".

Some people may be lucky they have their wishes, but having their wishes is not the result of having been born under the right star. It's the result of clarity, focus, passion, persistence and repeated effort. I wrote this book so that I could demystify this belief and give all of you, who have an idea, a dream or a personal project, the tools you need to make things happen for yourself. My sincere hope is that this book will teach you where to start, how to keep going and what to do when you hit some bumps along the way.

# About the method

The method has four parts and each of the parts is broken down into steps. It works for any desire, big or small. I've used it to make changes in large organisations but I've also used it to find the house of my dreams. You have absolute freedom on the end game. It's the structure I'm giving you that works. And for those of you who think structure stifles creativity, consider the following: all creative work involves structured activity. Whether it's painting or writing, the artist has to get up in the morning and work on their art *regularly* and *consistently*. In fact, one of the first things any "become a writer"-type book will teach you is that you have to set time aside for writing on a regular basis ideally each day. You can't just sit there and wish your book to appear, no matter how much you believe in the law of attraction (the name given to the belief that what you think about attracts what you want in your life). You have to follow a work pattern and do something and you have to deal with issues when they arise, for example keeping yourself motivated and ensuring the world knows about your art.

# Use structure as a tool

*"When forced to work within a framework the imagination is taxed to its utmost – and will produce its richest ideas. Given total freedom the work is likely to sprawl."*

*T.S. Eliot*

Structure creates momentum and focus. By knowing where you are headed, following a clearly laid plan or a set of steps, you are encouraged to take action. And take action in the right direction. You will make things happen faster because of it, as there will be no need to worry about what to do next. You will also know that all your energy is focused on the right type of activity. "Activity" that gets you closer to what you want rather than in the opposite direction. Let's say you want to build a house. You wouldn't go buy tons of materials before having decided what the house will look like, would you? If you did, you would not only waste money, you would waste your energy buying the wrong stuff. Instead, you would use your creativity to imagine the house of your dreams, then you would work out the layout and the materials you need. Then, you wouldn't start by building the roof, you would start by laying the foundation and you would build upon it.

Structure makes you more confident. It encourages you to get out there and do something rather than think about it for ages and become paralysed by fear. Attempting the exercise in bite-sized chunks increases your confidence. It breaks what you want to do into achievable steps. What, at first, seemed like an unbelievably large or scary undertaking now seems possible. Rome wasn't built in one day. Cliché but true. In fact, not much gets built in one day. If you deconstruct a project, you will find that it was small attempts, repeated regularly, that got the person there. Read the biographies of famous entrepreneurs like Richard Branson and Duncan Bannatyne and you will see that they took lots and lots of action before they got where they are today. It didn't always work the first time either, but all you see is the result, so you go "oh, aren't these people lucky". And what do you now know about lucky people?

Moving in increments also helps if you need to make adjustments to what you want or if you take the wrong turn. It's far easier to change and recover if the action was relatively small than if you'd bitten the whole project all at once. However clear you are about what you want, once you start making it real, the impact of the world and people around you may mean that you have some changes to make. The great product you thought the world needed might need some modifications before it starts selling like hot cakes. When you do something for real, it often turns out a little different from what is in your head and adjustments are part of the journey. So, from this point onwards, start thinking about the way to get what you want as a series of steps or tasks rather than one large jump into the unknown.

> *"It's a myth that change happens overnight, that right answers succeed in the marketplace right away, or that big ideas happen in a flash. They don't. It's always (almost always anyway) a matter of accretion. Drip, drip, drip."*
>
> *Seth Godin*

# Use structure to keep going

Structure keeps you accountable. Of course, you have to keep yourself accountable, but having steps to work through over a period of time creates context for accountability. Having an action plan that spans the next few months as a guide, and regularly measuring progress against that plan, moves you forward. It also ensures that you are working on all the relevant areas rather than only focusing on the tasks you find enjoyable. Let's say you want to change your lifestyle and you've decided this involves exercising, eating a healthier diet and spending time relaxing. You pull a plan together with actions that cover spending time in all three areas. Every day, you pull your plan out and you look at how to move towards your goal. Your plan reminds you to work on all three areas equally during the day or during the week. Now, consider a situation where you don't have a plan. You just make it up as you go along. The likelihood is that you will spend more time in the area you find easier or more enjoyable at the expense of the others. Or even in the area you hate the most, as you think this will make all the difference. Either way, you won't have a clear sense of direction and are likely to just end up "doing stuff" without a clear way to measure whether it's having a true impact and more importantly the right impact.

# Use structure to make your work seem like a journey

Structure will also make getting what you want in life seem like a journey. Think of the steps as phases on that journey. At each step, you develop new skills; you build on your progress and you move closer to your vision. Through the exercises, you develop the ability to focus on two things at once: the end game but also the present moment. Here's another secret: focusing on the end game is key as it drives you forward to the right place, but enjoying the journey and focusing your effort in the moment is also very important because if you hate the journey, you will be unlikely to put in the right level of effort and creative thinking. When I don't like doing something, I try to get through it as fast as I can. The problem with this is that I am then likely to miss some critical learning experience or even a new idea. Also, if I'm moaning all the way there, who is to say I won't be moaning when I get there? If what you want is right and exciting, and you are passionate about it, the journey there will be enjoyable. If the journey there isn't, you need to ask yourself if you are going after the right thing for the right reasons.

# Use structure to stay motivated

Structure allows you to notice progress. One way to definitely keep motivation and confidence up is to see the result of your efforts. Take an example where you've set yourself a goal of losing two pounds per week and you've decided to weigh yourself every Monday morning. Let's say you are succeeding and your efforts are paying off. Two pounds per week may not seem like much at first but it soon turns into four, six, eight and more. Once you get to half a stone (seven pounds), you will be very proud of your achievement and more likely to continue than if you had no way to track your progress. If you don't know how close to your goal you are getting, then remaining motivated will be very difficult. A word of caution: losing weight is hard for many people because there are often some emotional issues at play, so I'm not saying that you will succeed just by tracking progress. As explained below, tracking progress is one of the rational things you need to do, but you will also have to address your personal issues, the emotional side of getting what you want.

# Looking after the rational and the emotional

On top of offering structure, the method also encourages you to work on both the logical and the emotional aspects of getting what you want. On the logical side, there are steps for getting clear, steps for working out your plan and steps for putting that plan into action. These steps will appeal to the rational side of the brain. But ... it's not all about logic. There are also several steps that will help you deal with the key component of the journey to your vision: YOU. No plan in the world will work, however well crafted, if you are scared of getting your wish. If you don't think something is possible, you fear success or the voice inside your head keeps telling you that you won't succeed, then it won't matter how good your plan is. Even if I come to your house tomorrow and put the plan together myself, your subconscious will stop you from succeeding.

The aim is to align your subconscious with your conscious. To ensure that there aren't any demons lurking in your subconscious that will trip you over. I've used the word "demons" for effect. Whether you have demons, gremlins or small fairies in your subconscious, we will work together to raise them to awareness and figure out how to deal with them or enlist them for support. Getting distracted is one of my demons. Fortunately, I can be disciplined when I have to, and because I know I have a tendency to lose focus, I've learnt what to do to bring myself back on task. This is more a gremlin than a demon as it's not to do with a serious fear; it's to do with an overactive brain. What are your gremlins? Don't worry if you can't answer now; we will do it together later.

Unfortunately, you can't deal with the subconscious rationally. I can't give you a logical set of instructions: 1. Identify the fear; 2. Stop being scared. That won't work. What I can give you are tools and techniques to figure out what you are afraid of and to do something about it. Limiting beliefs, fears, lack of motivation and a whole array of other human factors influence your ability to change your current circumstances and make what you want happen. The "I don't have enough money", "I'm not clever enough" type of excuses keep you stuck where you are. You can do something about these things. People who get what they want are the proof. Read the story of any successful person to see that getting to where they are today involved them breaking through their limitations and fears to believe that achieving their vision was a possibility. This part of the book will appeal to your emotional side.

Because I've included techniques from a range of disciplines, the method is both rational and emotional and this is what makes it different. It helps you clarify what you want and figure out the path to get there but also how to deal with issues along the way.

# About the book

The book is organised around the method and each chapter is a step. Each of these steps teaches you a particular skill and encourages you to produce some outputs following the exercises. For example, you will be asked to develop a plan. Each chapter or step is a building block and there is a strong focus on doing. You can read the whole book once to get a "big picture" idea of the method. However, you will need to complete the exercises in the right order as they build on each other. Also, remember what we said about building confidence by breaking the journey to your desires into manageable chunks. Tackling one step at a time will help with that.

By following the steps in the book, you will:

- Understand the different elements that make up what you want and test them against your values (you'd be amazed how many people dream of things that entirely contradict what they hold dear)
- Develop a clear action plan
- Learn how obstacles (and emotional hang-ups) can kill motivation and what action can be taken to remove them
- Take small regular steps and make getting what you want an integral part of your daily life
- Build a support system and understand how to use it for help and to keep you on track
- Devise ways to measure your progress and continue applying the method once things start happening
- Learn what do to if things go wrong.

The focus is very much on learning through action and practice rather than just thinking about it. The aim is to get you working, and you can complete the exercises on paper or electronically. The worksheets are available from my website at www.brigittecobb.com or you can create your own. It's not important what they look like; the content is what is important so if you want to make them look different, go right ahead.

# About what you want

To use the book, you need to know what you want. I haven't included steps in this book to discover what that is; I'm assuming you already know. If you don't know and the issue is that you feel you could be or have more of something, then I suggest you get some coaching to work through your feelings and clarify what would make you happy. Then come back and I will help you make it happen.

The method will work for any project, big or small. What may be different is the depth you need to get into, which will get clearer as you do the exercises. For example, if you want to lose weight, your plan will obviously include fewer tasks than if you are building an extension to your house; but it may take longer. However, in both cases, you will still need to have a plan. The essence of the exercises will remain the same.

You can use the book for personal or professional hopes, wishes, projects and dreams. Whether you want to retire early or set up a home business, the method will work. However, as I said earlier, to get started, you need to have a good idea of what you want. Just knowing that you want to start a business is not going to work with this book; you have to know what type of business. Then you can use the method to test your idea, research it and make it happen. However, there is little business advice in here, so you will also need to buy yourself some reference books on accounting, marketing, sales, etc., or to get advice from someone who is in business already.

# Action and commitment

Once you are clear on what you want, you can complete the exercises in any way you like (on paper, electronically, by drawing your answers) but you will need to produce some "physical" outputs. Just thinking up the answers in your head won't work because we will keep referring to previous exercises as well as building on them. Also, psychologically it's good to have a physical representation of your work. It sends a message to the world and more importantly to yourself that you are serious about this. If you think about it, what we are trying to do is materialise what you want for yourself, so make sure that the first thing you practise bringing into reality is the work you do on the exercises. As your first task and sign of commitment to your project, why don't you go this week and buy yourself a workbook? You will also need a diary if you haven't got one already.

As a second sign of commitment, you will also need to dedicate the time to read the chapters and complete the exercises – in the right order. Your desires will not become reality without action. Although I believe that you can make things happen by setting your mind to it, I know for a fact that just thinking about your vision positively and wishing it were yours will not work unless you take action. At this point, I would like you to make a conscious decision and ask yourself: how much time will you dedicate to your project? A good rule of thumb would be about an hour each time you pick up the book and you'd need to pick up the book on a regular basis, so we are not looking for an hour every day (it's actually good to have breaks to reflect); we are probably looking for something like an hour, two to three times a week.

If you cannot make blocks of one-hour commitments, think of smaller focused blocks of time you could fit in. Could you get up 30 minutes earlier? How about giving up some TV time in the evening?

Whatever you decide, book the time in your diary as a real appointment and ensure that nothing will distract your focus (more about distraction later). Even lots of 10-minute blocks are better than nothing. I wrote this book whilst in a full-time job where I had to travel an hour to get to the office and an hour to get back and also ensure I spent time with my husband and kids. I even managed to fit in some regular Pilates and coaching sessions. How did I do it? At first I tried to write whenever I could, but this didn't work very well as some weeks I did nothing. Things took off when I booked a regular three-hour session each Sunday morning. Yes, it took me about a year to complete the project, but isn't that better than having just sat there thinking "Three hours a week? Wow! That's going to take too long." The reality is that I didn't think about it that way, I really enjoyed my three hours of writing and each week I felt good about the journey as well as about getting closer to my goal. And between sessions I spent the time reading about change, talking to people, having ideas and making notes.

As a third sign of commitment, you will also need to keep yourself on track. If you're not good at staying on track then consider hiring a coach, finding a buddy or engaging your support system. We will discuss this more later. For now, just get started.

There is a companion website to go with the book. The address is www.brigittecobb.com; you can use the website to:

- Download worksheets
- Take a look at some worked examples
- Participate in discussions
- Sign up for workshops or coaching
- Find additional resources.

# The method

At the front of the book is a graphical representation of the method. Download a copy from the website, print it and post it on the wall. You'll then be able to track where you are using a pin or a sticker. For extra motivation, you can put a tick mark next to the steps you have already completed.

# And remember...

*"Vision without action is merely a dream. Action without vision just passes the time. Vision with action can change the world."*

*Joel A. Barker*

# Come on. Let's fly!

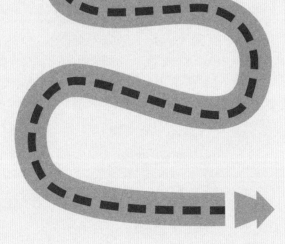

PART **1**
DEFINE, REFINE
AND MAKE IT REAL

**1** Decide what's in and what's out
**2** Is what you want right for you?
**3** Paint a compelling picture
**4** Make it real, tell the world

# PART 1

## Define, refine and make it real

"Success is getting what you want. Happiness is wanting what you get."

Dale Carnegie

So what is it that you want? And will you be happy when you get it? In this section, I will help you clarify your goals, figure out if what you want is right for you, learn to visualise and start telling the world that you are serious about this.

# Step 1

## Decide what's in and what's out

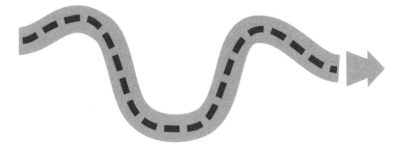

"*The reason most people never reach their goals is that they don't define them, or ever seriously consider them as believable or achievable. Winners can tell you where they are going, what they plan to do along the way, and who will be sharing the adventure with them.*"

Denis Waitley

To move forward in the right direction requires a certain amount of clarity. If you don't know where you are headed, how can you be motivated about the future? A clear vision will excite you and pull you forward regardless of the obstacles life puts in your way. This vision will also act as your guide. On top of driving you forward, it will help you define the right actions to take to get your goals. If you are taking action without a clear vision, how will you know that you are putting your energies and resources in the right place? And, actually, how can you make sure you'll end up in the right place?

# Creating experiences or getting something?

Let's say that what you want is to live in a bigger house. If we were working together, I would ask you to clarify what this bigger house would look like, how much bigger it would be. I would also be keen to understand the type of experiences you are trying to create from getting a bigger house. Do you wish to create more space for your family to grow, or is this about status and comfort? Visions are typically related to creating an experience rather than creating "things". The path to get there is typically where you will find the "things" needed to achieve that experience. For example, using the right questions, we may find that your wish isn't about having a bigger house; it really is about increasing your status. In that case, we could make your vision to be "increasing your status" rather than "having a bigger house" and define the action plan as a series of mini-projects aimed at enhancing status, for example buy a nicer car, get promoted and have a bigger house.

# Your vision can be flexible

The point is that whilst your vision has to be clear, it can remain flexible and it will be if you are describing an experience. This is useful since typically you will not be able to completely plan what will happen once you get what you want. Once your vision starts taking shape, events, other people, your experiences, may force you to adapt. If you feel that what you want really isn't an experience and you have been dreaming for years of a bigger house and you can picture it clearly in your mind, then it's perfectly fine to make your vision about a "thing". It's your wishes and desires, always remember that.

# Use your vision as a guide

The point is that whatever the vision, you need to be able to use it to test that the projects (that's what we will call a bunch of actions that take you to a common thing) you add to your plan stand a good chance of getting you there. It is important that you can answer whether taking action A will get you to your goal or whether you would be better off taking action B as this will actually be more fun and more aligned to your personality and will get you there faster.

# Mini-projects need control and are not as flexible

We said that your vision could be about an experience and offer you some flexibility of approach. The projects, on the other hand, must be crystal clear before you take serious action. In the above example, if you decide that getting a bigger house is about creating space, you would become clear on the project aimed at building an extension before you start knocking down walls. Otherwise, you could waste time, energy and money knocking down the wrong walls. It is possible to change a project once you've started; however, it would be preferable to do so when you are initially defining it (in the planning phase). In fact, I am actually expecting that the more you work through Parts 1 and 2 of the book and reflect, the more you may need to adjust your vision and projects so that they are just right for you by the time we get to really take action. So, take your time with the exercises. As we said earlier, it is also important that you describe what you want on paper so that we have somewhere to start and a reference point to come back to once you progress in your work (who knows, you may grow in confidence and end up with a really big dream).

# Short term vs long term

An easy way to think of the vision, the projects and the action you'll be taking is to categorise them as short term, medium term or long term. In the example of the house, you could create more space in a variety of ways: de-clutter, extend or move. What if what you ultimately want is to move but there is urgency to create space this year and you can only afford to de-clutter and possibly build an extension? This is where being able to balance short-term/medium-term (projects) and long-term plans (vision) can help.

This step is about deciding on your long-term goal. In our example, your long-term goal is to move to a bigger house in a more affluent neighbourhood to create an experience where you get more space but also increase your status. But you know that realistically, you won't be able to do that until you have paid 50% of your existing mortgage. So, you decide to take some more short-term steps to create space. You decide to break your vision into three phases: short, medium and long term. In Phase I (short term), you will de-clutter the spare room and create a new study. In Phase II (medium term), you will build an extension, but in Phase III (longer term) you will move. It is up to you to define the number of months or years that relate to each phase. In this example, let's say that Phase I is a three-month period, Phase II is between one and two years and Phase III is around five years.

Here's a graphical representation of the above:

| Vision | Phase I – 3 months | Phase II – 1 to 2 years | Phase III – 5 years |
|---|---|---|---|
| Move to a bigger house to create space. Experience: increase status and comfort | De-clutter the spare room and create a new study | Build an extension | Move |

# Structure and long-term thinking

What structure and long-term thinking help with is making sure that the decisions you make now do not contradict the end game. So in this example, you would need to think carefully whether the investment in a new study and extension would help you reach your ultimate goal. This will depend on your circumstances and you'll need to model different scenarios, but it is likely that having a nice study and an extension would add value to your house and may make sense when you come to sell it in five years' time. Nevertheless, you'd have to make sure that you don't end up investing too much and you are still in a position to pay 50% of the mortgage before the five years are up. Having a vision will help you align the short-term plans so that you end up where you want in the end. If you find balancing short-, medium- and long-term plans too complicated or what you want is simple, then my advice is to have only one end state at a time, for example to move house in the next six months.

# Structure what you want

What we are doing is structuring what you want so that you have a vision and that this vision is broken down into different components or projects. It's probably best now to have a go at the exercise below and see where that gets you. One very important point here: don't go for perfection the first time you complete one of the exercises. They all build on each other so you will end up "perfecting" your goals throughout Parts 1 and 2.

# Make it fly

Here's what I'd like you to do. Check your diary and make sure you can spend time doing this exercise uninterrupted. It is important that the exercises are completed in order, otherwise the method will not yield the anticipated results. The method is a building-block approach where you lay the foundation and then add to it. You need to start with the right blocks.

This exercise will help you brainstorm and by the time you are done, you will know what you want, why you want it and your aims and objectives. You will also make a start on what is included and what isn't. What isn't included can be important because these are the things that you are committing to spending zero energy on. In the words of American philanthropist Elbert Hubbard: *"Many people fail in life, not for lack of ability or brains or even courage, but simply because they have never organised their energies around a goal."* And I would add, around the "right goal".

You will need about 20 to 30 minutes, pen and paper or a computer, and a binder or workbook to collate your work.

The exercise asks you to make your objectives SMART if you can. This means ensuring that they are:

**S**  Specific

**M**  Measurable

**A**  Attainable

**R** Relevant

**T** Time-bound

So instead of saying:

"Objective 1: To move to a bigger house"

You say:

"Objective 1: To move to a brand-new five-bedroom house with three reception rooms and a large garden in neighbourhood xyz by the 1st of July 2016"

As it's still early days, you may not be able to make your objectives SMART yet because you have some research to do. That's fine. We'll do it later.

I won't repeat this enough: *don't* try to be perfect, just *do it*!

Now, your turn.

---

### STEP 1 EXERCISE

### SCOPE AND OBJECTIVES

1. Describe what you want in as much detail as you can. What is your vision? What experiences are you trying to create?
2. Why do you want this? What is the purpose? What will you get that you haven't got now?
3. What is your aim? What are your objectives? Can you make your objectives SMART?
4. What is included and what is not included?

---

When you've completed the scope and objectives exercise, print it out and insert it in your workbook or binder.

# Step 2

# Is what you want right for you?

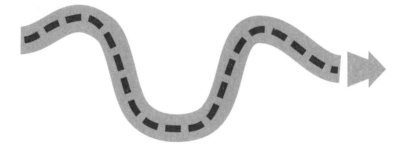

*"Just as your car runs more smoothly and requires less energy to go faster and farther when the wheels are in perfect alignment, you perform better when your thoughts, feelings, emotions, goals, and values are in balance."*

Brian Tracy

Your personal values drive you. They are aspects of life, qualities or concepts that you hold dear and you subconsciously (or consciously) use to make decisions and remain motivated. Typically, achievements that align with your values make you happy. Here are some examples: family, charity, excellence and health. There is a comprehensive list in the exercise at the end of this step.

## Where do values come from?

We ultimately chose our values. However, many of our values come from our childhood and family environment. The messages we receive from our parents and the experiences we have form our values. This may mean adopting the same value system as our parents, or it may mean the opposite: think of the straight-laced parents and the rebel child.

Some of our values will be deeply held and won't change; however, our experiences as we grow up and our life stages will have an influence. You may have been an idealist who wanted to change the world in your student years, but life as a nine-to-fiver in an office may have changed all that (or maybe not!). The culture of your country will also have an impact. I emigrated in my early 20s and I am now a mix of my former country culture and my adopted country culture. This has opened my eyes to how much impact national culture has on us. Meal times in my house are interesting; I come from a culture where meal times are all about socialising and there isn't much etiquette. In my adopted country, it's different. There are rules on how to hold your knife and fork, rules on when to start, rules on when to talk. I think my husband and I have made the best of both worlds but my children have funny experiences, as they have to behave differently at home (average amount of rules) and at school (more rules). I guess this is what makes life interesting and people more rounded.

## Aligning your values to what you want

Any dream you have, change you wish to make or goal you set that isn't aligned to your value system is unlikely to succeed. Or if it does, it will probably not make you very happy. If what you want clashes with your values, you will feel conflicted and will struggle to stay motivated. Here's an example: I hold "family" high on my value list and it is important for me to spend quality time with my family every day. I also naturally put them first and I have never spent a holiday without my children. Some of my friends go on two-week holidays without their children and don't understand that I want to take my family with me. I find them strange and they find me strange; we have a different value system. This means that I need a job where I get home relatively early and I am not away for weeks on end. So, an ambition of finding a job as a travelling saleswoman would not be a good idea because I would be away from home all the time. I know this is a little obvious as an example but you get the point. As we discussed, your values and priorities may change, so it is important that you complete the values exercise if you have not done one in the last year or so. For example, family was less important to me when I was 25, single and had no children.

# Leveraging your values

On the positive side, if your vision is aligned to your values, you will be naturally motivated and you will feel good about yourself. Your values will drive you forward. My value of freedom is the reason why I am self-employed. I have tried working for other people and I get really unhappy. A salaried job makes me feel trapped. I like self-employment because it has limitless possibilities; I can change what I do any time I like and if I provide a good service or product, there is the opportunity to earn a good living. My visions have often been about creating experiences where there's lots of freedom.

# Make it fly

To assess if what you want is right for you and to make sure you will be fully motivated to work on it come what may, complete the values exercise below. There are two exercises in this step. The first one is to discover your values and the second one is to compare against what you want. If you don't have enough time, you can, if you wish, complete the value exercise now and come back to assess against your vision in your next session. Each exercise is likely to take 15 to 20 minutes to complete.

You will need pen and paper or a computer, your binder or workbook. Once you have completed the second exercise, print out the sheet and insert it in your binder or workbook.

# STEP 2 EXERCISE (PART 1)
# IDENTIFY YOUR VALUES

The aim of the exercise is to list 10 values in order of importance. We will do this exercise in two parts.

In the first part, look at the values in the table below and, as a first step, strike out any that are not important to you and circle all the ones that are. It is likely that you will end up with more than 10 words circled. Don't worry, we will address this in the second part of the exercise.

| | | | |
|---|---|---|---|
| Achievement | Freedom | Knowledge | Security |
| Adventure | Free time | Leadership | Self-awareness |
| Affluence | Friendship | Learning | Self-discipline |
| Beauty | Fun | Love | Self-esteem |
| Challenge | Gratitude | Mastery | Self-expression |
| Charity | Growth | Nature | Self-respect |
| Collaboration | Guaranteed income | Nurturing | Sensitivity |
| Commitment | Happiness | Open mindedness | Services |
| Community | Harmony | Order | Social intelligence |
| Compassion | Health | Partnership | Spirituality |
| Courage | Honesty | Peace | Stimulation |
| Creativity | Humility | Perseverance | Strength |
| Curiosity | Humour | Personal | Success |
| Dignity | Independence | development | Supportiveness |
| Elegance | Individuality | Pleasure | Talent |
| Empowerment | Influence | Power | Teamwork |
| Energy | Integrity | Pride | Trust |
| Enjoyment | Intimacy | Prudence | Truth |
| Excellence | Inventiveness | Reason | Wellbeing |
| Exercise | Justice | Recognition | Wisdom |
| Family | Kindness | Risk | |

Now take your reduced list. You'll notice that some values are very similar, for example honesty, integrity and truth. If you have such groups of values circled, look to see which one is truly important to you and see if you can strike out the others.

List your remaining values in a grid like the one below, making sure that each value appears both horizontally and vertically. For example, Affluence appears here in the column on the left but also in the top row. (Please note that the picture below is a cut-down version of the values you are likely to be left with. When you set up your grid, please make sure all remaining values appear both along the top and down the left-hand side.)

| | Affluence | Challenge | Energy | Exercise | Enjoyment |
|---|---|---|---|---|---|
| Affluence | | | | | |
| Challenge | | | | | |
| Energy | | | | | |
| Exercise | | | | | |
| Enjoyment | | | | | |

Once your grid is set up, take each value in the column on the left and compare it to each value at the top, asking yourself which one is more important. Then write the one that is more important in the box. See below for an example, where 'achievement' is more important than 'challenge', 'creativity' and 'excellence' but less important than 'family'.

| | Achievement | Challenge | Creativity | Excellence | Family |
|---|---|---|---|---|---|
| Achievement | | Achievement | Achievement | Achievement | Family |
| Challenge | | Learning | Challenge | Excellence | Family |
| Creativity | | | | Creativity | Family |
| Excellence | | | | | Family |
| Family | | | | | |

In essence, it is a matter of comparing the values against each other until you end up with a list of 10. Once you have your list of 10, you will need to sort them in order of importance. Once again, you can achieve this by comparing one to the other. Make sure you also make a note of your 'secondary' values, that is, the five that come after your top 10.

When you have your list of 10 top values and your five secondary values, print it out and glue them to your workbook.

In the second part of the exercise, we will take your value list and assess how it may conflict with what you want or could be used to support it.

You will need 15 to 20 minutes, pen and paper or a computer, your binder or scrapbook (glue, dividers, hole punch, etc.).

### STEP 2 EXERCISE (PART 2)

## ASSESS YOUR VISION AGAINST YOUR VALUES

Take the output from the exercise in Step 1 and your list of values from Step 2 above. Reading both several times, answer the following questions:

1. Which of your top 10 values would support your goals? For example, health would be a good value if what you want is to improve your lifestyle.

2. Which of the values you haven't chosen would be necessary for getting what you want? Is this going to be a challenge? How could you meet this challenge? How far from your set of values is the missing value?

3. Which of your top 10 values would contradict your vision?

4. What is the strength of this contradiction? Is this only a small issue or is it a big issue?

5. Having done the analysis, how do you feel? Is what you want still right for you? Do you need to make some adjustments?

# Step 3

# Paint a compelling picture

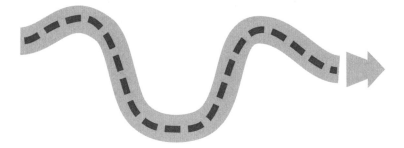

*"Big thinking precedes big achievement."*
Wilfred Peterson

In Steps 1 and 2, we've done some work to define what you want and to assess this against your values. In Step 3, you will start to picture your end goal in your mind (and hopefully get really excited about the possibilities). To do this, we will use what you have developed to date and turn it into a vision. You will then be able to use this vision for motivation and to propel you forward. This vision will describe what the world will look like when you get what you want. Hopefully, when you create your vision and when you see it, you will feel excited and full of energy. It will be colourful, big and bold. Your vision will engage all of your senses and you will also be able to touch it, hear it and feel it.

# Use your vision to start uncovering challenges

Your vision may also indirectly help you identify challenges. Here's how this may happen. You've developed a wonderful picture of what you're after but you don't seem to find 15 minutes in your day to focus on it and keep yourself motivated. You, strangely, keep forgetting to do this exercise. This points to an issue because if you really want something, you would remember to do it. Right? Or maybe, you do remember to visualise for 15 minutes every day but when you bring your wonderful vision to mind, you keep trying to tone it down. The colours are too bright, the noises are too loud, you're doing too well. You don't feel quite right about reaching your goals. This points to issues of confidence. And the trouble is that if you don't feel comfortable picturing what you want in all its glory, the chances are you won't feel comfortable with it becoming real. What these feelings are telling you is that there are some emotional issues to discover and work through. We will spend a lot of time in Part 3 working on limitations, but for now just make a note of what comes up for you.

# Oh no, I don't believe I can get what I want

In order for you to make things happen, your conscious and unconscious have to align and work together. You have to consciously and unconsciously want to reach your goals. If your unconscious doesn't believe what you want to be possible, it will put all sorts of clever obstacles in your path. It may distract you, make you forget to work on your project or even in some cases make you ill. Yes, that's right, it's that strong.

If your unconscious and your conscious minds are aligned, your vision of what you want will feel wonderful, it will motivate you and it will be something you regularly bring into focus during the day. I would suggest performing your visualisation exercise every morning when you get up and every night before sleep (if there are people around and you feel embarrassed, just do it in the shower or close your eyes on the train to work). Your vision will also be very useful every time something de-motivates you or you face an obstacle; bringing it into mind will help lessen the negative feelings arising from the obstacle and give you courage to overcome it.

# Now develop your vision

What you want to end up with is a clear picture in your mind of what the world will look like once you've reached your ultimate end goal. Although it is called a "vision", it is important that you engage all your senses in the exercise. I'd like you to be able to see, touch, hear and feel what being there will be like. If you want to be an actress, picture yourself on the stage performing or at drama school perfecting your skills. Hear the crowd, feel how you will feel. If what you want is to write a book, picture your book sitting on the shelf of the local bookstore and yourself sitting at a table signing copies for your readers. Hear your readers asking for autographs, feel how this will feel.

# Make it fly

So let's have a go at creating your vision. You will need 15 to 20 minutes and a quiet place where you won't be disturbed and you can close your eyes.

### STEP 3 EXERCISE

## CREATE YOUR VISION

- Find a location where you won't be disturbed. Take the phone off the hook and find a comfortable chair, ideally with a straight back. Sit down, lean your back against the chair, put your feet firmly on the floor and close your eyes.

- Relax your entire body, starting with your feet. The technique is simply to run through your body from feet to face, clenching and releasing each area. So, first clench your toes then relax them, then clench your feet and relax them, then clench your lower legs and relax them and so on and so on, until you scrunch up your face and relax it.

- If you don't like the clenching thing, you could use breathing. Breathe in counting to 7 and out counting to 7 and repeat seven times. Use whatever works best for you as a relaxation technique. Do this slowly; if you do it too quickly, your head may spin.

- When you are relaxed, create an image of what you want in your mind. Make the image big and the colours bold and bright.

- Hear the sounds you will be hearing when you get what you want (the audience applauding your performance?).

- Feel how you will feel in that situation (a warm feeling of achievement? excited?).

- If what you want has a taste, also taste it (not that easy with the acting thing but appropriate if you are opening a restaurant or cooking for a major event).

- If touch and smell are appropriate, throw that in as well (maybe as an actress you get a bunch of flowers at the end of the performance and you can touch and smell them).

- Go on. Let your imagination loose. Try to give the picture as real a feel as you can. And have some fun.

- You will know you are succeeding if you get a lot of energy in your body.

- Before you complete the exercise, try to notice the feelings in your body so that you can easily recreate them. For me, energy lives in the chest. When I'm energised and motivated, my chest is wide open, my shoulders are pushed back and I have a feeling of abundance. I can picture a flow of light coming out of my chest. Excitement, on the other hand, tingles all over and I feel tall and on top of the world. I feel possibility in my abdomen.

- Once you can really feel your vision and you are happy with the results, slowly come back into your body and open your eyes.

# Step 4

## Make it real, tell the world

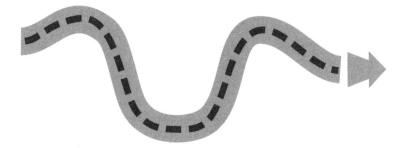

"How many times in your life have you said you were going to do something, and then not done it because nobody else would know the difference? Just the simple act of telling your plan to another person raises the stakes. On a freezing January morning, you might pull the covers back over your head rather than go to the health club alone. But if you've promised to meet someone there at 7:00 a.m., there is a much better chance you'll actually get your chilly butt out of bed and go."

Laura Wintworth

In this step, I will help you start to slowly move what you want from a thought in your head to reality. We will do this by sharing your vision with people. Telling your family and friends that you are working on a special project is a big step, but doing so is likely to have the following effects:

- Speaking out requires you to have some level of confidence that your idea can effectively come to fruition, so by the time you do so, you will know you have reached that place where you feel it is possible.

- Sharing your vision is likely to get you some constructive feedback, which you can use to refine your goals. Do be careful, though, as some people may be negative just because they haven't got the courage to move their own projects forward or they are frightened that your proposed change will affect their relationship with you. For example, your partner and close family may worry that you becoming slim may stop them enjoying sumptuous meals. You will need to be the judge of what is constructive criticism and what is simply criticism. Just thank the person for the comment and reflect on it to see whether you also believe that to be true. If you do, you will get a great opportunity to further develop your idea.

- Telling will also help to build your commitment to act; obviously, if none of the people you speak to hold you accountable then this may have limited effect, but this depends. Simply telling that you're heading in a certain direction and having people regularly ask how you're doing may encourage you to keep moving forward. It may also highlight an issue if you're not making progress.

We'll look at commitment and motivation in Parts 3 and 4; at this early stage, all I am suggesting is that you start telling people to move your idea from a thought to reality, get some good feedback to refine your vision and start building momentum by having regular discussions about your plans.

# The day I shared my vision with people

I started thinking about this book three years before I completed the first draft. At first, I didn't tell anyone, but as I pulled the method into a diagram and brainstormed titles, I grew in confidence and I told my husband. He didn't really know about publishing books but he encouraged me to find someone who could give me some advice. I trailed the Internet and I found someone advertising as a writing consultant and coach. I made an appointment and told this lady what I wanted to do. It all took off from there. I got great advice from her and she taught me how to pull a proposal together and approach publishers. The point is that had I not told my husband, he wouldn't have suggested that I look for advice and I may not have looked for a coach. I may have spent the next year thinking of going for it rather than taking action, because I didn't really know how books got published.

But so that you don't think my life is always flowing brilliantly without hiccups, here's a not so great example of telling people. During the year and a half I spent writing the first draft, I told many people about my book. The more I wrote, the more fun I was having and the more confident I felt. I was told more than once that publishing a book was really hard, that I needed a platform or nobody would sign me up, that so-and-so had tried and failed. I chose to ignore those comments because I knew my method worked, I was really enjoying writing the book and I thought there was no way something I loved doing so much wasn't going to get out there. In any case, my writing coach had advised me that if I couldn't find a publisher, I could always self-publish and that seemed interesting as well. At the end of the day, what I wanted was to help people by getting my ideas out in the world; I reasoned that there was more than one way to do that. I was confident, so it was easier to ignore demotivating comments, but do be careful! Your vision is precious; be prepared to use your ability to discern useful from negative.

# Make it fly

So let's make a commitment to telling some people by creating a small action plan. You will need 15 to 20 minutes, pen and paper or a computer, your binder or workbook (glue, dividers, hole punch, etc.).

> **STEP 4 EXERCISE**
>
> **TELL PEOPLE**
>
> First, decide what you would like to get from telling people about your vision and your goals. Some examples may be:

- Confidence: become more confident about describing your plans to someone else.

- Feedback: get some constructive feedback so that you can refine your ideas, clarify your goals, test the viability of a business dream, etc.

- Accountability: help with starting to feel accountable.

Second, make a list of people you'd like to tell, and next to their names write whether you'd like them to help with confidence, accountability, feedback or something else.

Then write out a date by which you will talk to them. This is your first mini action plan!

**PART 2**
**PLAN AND PLAN**
**AGAIN**

**5** Define your approach
**6** Create a first cut of your plan
**7** Make sure you have what you need
**8** Finalise your plan
**9** Identify your success partners

# PART 2

## Plan and plan again

*"A fool with a plan is better off than a genius without a plan!"*

T. Boone Pickens

In Part 1, you worked on defining your vision and goals and started making what you wanted real by telling people. In Part 2, we will define the strategy you will use for getting what you want. Your strategy will include the approach you will take, the plan you will follow, the resources you will require and how you can use success partners to encourage and support you along the way.

# Step 5

# Define your approach

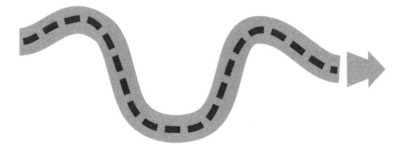

*"What do you want to achieve or avoid? The answers to this question are objectives. How will you go about achieving your desired results? The answer to this you can call strategy."*

William E. Rothschild

Your approach is the first component of your strategy. It consists in defining how you will bridge the gap between where you are now and where you want to be. It is the type of action you'll choose to take to reach your objectives. There are lots of ways to achieve the same thing, but what is the best way for you? Think about what you want to create; better still, get hold of your Step 1 exercise. Consider where you are now, then compare it to where you want to be. What is the gap between the two? How do you want to plug that gap? What are all the areas you'll need to work on? Are there ways of getting there you just don't like? Are there ways of getting there that will be faster than others?

# Let's use an example

Let's say you want to change your lifestyle, and the experience you want to create is to feel great and to live longer. As your goals, you may have written that you wish to lose 15 lbs over the next three months, that you will tone and strengthen your body (and you may have added detail on which areas you want to focus on) and that you will cut down your level of stress by half. I'm sure you'll agree, there is more than one way to get to these goals, and some of these ways will appeal more to you than others. Some ways will also work better for you. It would therefore be useful to brainstorm the different ways and pick the ones that will be most effective rather than go down a path that may be less fun, be slower to yield results or even require more effort. Let's illustrate this point by taking each of the goals in the previous example and coming up with different approaches for each of them (see the table below).

# Brainstorm even if you know your approach

It only took me a few minutes to come up with different ways to reach each of the above objectives. If I were to spend another 10 minutes, I'm sure I'd come up with some more. Doing this is what I mean by "developing your approach". Even if you already know what approach you will take to reach each of your goals, I would still like you to complete the exercise. There are two reasons for this: firstly, I would like your approach to be

| Goal | Possible Approaches |
|------|---------------------|
| Lose 1 stone (6 kg) over the next 3 months | • Join a slimming club<br>• Consult a nutritionist and get a menu written up<br>• Join a gym that can develop a combined exercise and eating programme for me |
| Tone and strengthen my body | • Join a gym and get a programme developed<br>• Purchase some gym equipment and set it up in my spare room<br>• Buy a bike and cycle to work every day<br>• Swim twice per week<br>• Join a Pilates class |
| Reduce stress by 50% in the next 6 months | • Make sure I take my full lunch break and get away from my desk every day<br>• Leave work on time<br>• Learn to meditate and do it for 20 minutes every day<br>• Do at least one relaxing thing every night before I go to bed e.g. read, have a bath, etc. |

recorded on paper so that it is real and we can use it to develop an action plan; secondly, if unfortunately the first approach you select doesn't work, then you can come back to this exercise and choose one of the alternatives, or, even better, maybe you can combine some of the approaches.

We can also use this exercise to ensure that you don't miss out any aspects of what you want. Think of our lifestyle example. Are there any other ways to "feel healthier and live longer" than the ones mentioned above? I was at a seminar recently where Janey Lee Grace (www.imperfectlynatural. com) introduced us to the idea that the cleaning products in our houses may be making us sick. I'd heard this concept before but never did anything about it. Her talk and her examples got me thinking that it may be time to put the effort in and make a change. So, based on this, I could add the following objective to the previous example: "making my house a healthier environment to live in", and choose an approach where I throw out all the harsh cleaning products in favour of environmentally friendly ones.

# How having an approach can help with challenges

During the research for this book I spoke to several people about their ambitions. One of these people is my friend Vicky. Vicky has a clear vision: she wants to use her passion for make-up to offer impartial advice to people. She feels most advice you can currently get is geared towards particular brands, in effect limiting choices. She sees lots of opportunities and has started getting some bookings. She's very fired up about this. But ... when I ask her how well it's going, her energy dips. Even with a clear and exciting vision, she is progressing very slowly. Vicky tells me that she is really struggling to find time to work on her project. She has three young children and a part-time job and can't fit much in. With a few questions, I discover that she does have a regular slot on Thursday mornings, but without an approach and a plan she often fails to make the best of her precious time as she sits there wondering what to do next rather than taking action. If, like Vicky, time is a challenge, your approach can help focus your time and energy. Think how much faster you'd progress if you were clear where to put your efforts. (For more information on Vicky, you can find her at www. victoriajolliffe.co.uk.)

# Make it fly

You will be developing your approach in a couple of stages. First, we'll brainstorm methods you could use to achieve your goals, then we will assess where you are currently with respect to your goals and select the approaches that will work best for you. Make sure you have the time to do the exercise and get hold of what you need to complete it.

---

### STEP 5 EXERCISE (PART 1)

### IDENTIFY YOUR APPROACH

1. Get hold of your Step 1 exercise and read the content.
2. Take your objectives and your scope items, whichever makes sense to break into an approach.

---

3. Build a table like the one in the previous example and have a good brainstorm at several ways you could achieve your goals or reach your objectives.

4. Don't stress about doing this exercise perfectly, just *do it*!

As you develop your approach, you may notice that it's starting to resemble a plan. Don't worry if it does, in fact this is good, as we will then use the exercises in this step to start building your plan in Step 6.

In order to complete the last exercise, you will have had to start thinking of where you are on the way to your vision so that you can think of activities that will get you there. Although you may feel assessing where you are has already been done, my recommendation is that we document this through an exercise for the following reasons:

- In order to measure progress, we need to know the starting point.

- If you have already completed some activities, we can then mark them as "in progress".

- Assessing where you are may lead you to rework your approach.

Make sure you have the time to do the exercise and get hold of what you need to complete it.

## STEP 5 EXERCISE (PART 2)

## REFINE YOUR APPROACH BY ASSESSING WHERE YOU ARE

- Get hold of the exercise you completed previously (Step 5 – Part 1) and add a third column to the right of the table. Call the new column 'Assess Current State' to signify where you are now.

- For each goal or scope item, write down where you are with respect to where you want to be. Have a look at the example below for guidance.

| Goal | Possible Approaches | Assess Current State |
|------|---------------------|----------------------|
| Lose 1 stone (6 kg) over the next 3 months | • Join a slimming club<br>• Consult a nutritionist and get a menu written up<br>• Join a gym that can develop a combined exercise and eating programme for me | • I currently weigh 10 stone (63.5 kg). In order to have a good BMI for my height, I should weigh 9 stone (57 kg).<br>• My diet is good but my portions are too big. I don't really snack between meals, which is good and bad as it means my sugar levels often drop, making me irritable.<br>• My back hurts from the excess weight that I'm carrying around. |
| Tone and strengthen my body | • Join a gym and get a programme developed<br>• Purchase some gym equipment and set it up in my spare room<br>• Buy a bike and cycle to work every day<br>• Swim twice per week<br>• Join a Pilates class | • I'm really out of shape and I get out of breath going up more than one flight of stairs.<br>• My lower back hurts because my abdominal muscles are weak.<br>• My shoulders hurt regularly from sitting at a desk all day and I struggle to sleep on my left side. |
| Reduce stress by 50% in the next 6 months | • Make sure I take my full lunch break and get away from my desk every day<br>• Leave work on time<br>• Learn to meditate and do it for 20 minutes every day<br>• Do at least one relaxing thing every night before I go to bed e.g. read, have a bath, etc. | • I never take a lunch break, which is not good as I get no fresh air and no sun during the weekdays.<br>• I currently work 50 hours per week, which is probably not that productive, really stressful and means I feel guilty for not spending enough time with my family.<br>• I don't spend enough time reflecting as I'm always running from one thing to the next.<br>• NOTE: Just writing this made me feel stressed! |

As I mentioned before, "assessing current state" may have made you realise that you need to change your approach: please go ahead and do so as you work through the exercises.

# Step 6

# Create a first cut of your plan

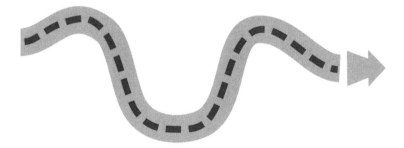

*"Goals are dreams we convert to plans and take action to fulfil."*

Zig Ziglar

If your approach is the way you will get to your goals and eventually to your vision, your plan is the list of actions you will need to take to get there. Remember how we talked about using structure to break down what you want? If you have done the work and completed the exercises, you will be starting to see structure around your vision. Your objectives, goals and approaches will be giving your vision a shape and hopefully making it feel achievable and within reach.

What we don't have yet is a detailed list of actions. This is where this step comes in. As you worked through the previous exercises, you will have started to think about the actions you'll need to take. For example, if losing weight is one of your goals and joining a slimming club is how you want to go about it, you may have already started enquiring about slimming clubs in your area. This is called taking action.

# The law of attraction

In recent years, "the law of attraction" has gained in popularity through several books and films and much has been written about the impact of our thoughts on reality. The theory is that what you think about is what you attract, so if you think of a life full of challenges, this is what you'll get. I can tell you from experience that this is true. I picked up my first positive thinking book when I was 27 years old and my life was never the same again. In the space of about 12 months, I significantly improved my working life by finding the courage to change my job and then to become self-employed. However ... a word of caution. Many books on the law of attraction seem to imply that you can sit at home and wish for the best, and the best will come. I find that as far as I'm concerned, I also need to *take action*. So in the example of improving my working life, I had to be willing to change job twice, to believe I deserved to be paid more, and to be on the lookout for opportunities, then to grab them with both hands when they came along. Based on my experience with the law of attraction and positive thinking, you need to do both: have the right thoughts *and* take action. The plan we will develop in this step will help you take action. The vision that we developed in Step 3 and the work we will do on limiting beliefs and fears later on will help you have the right thoughts.

# Let's develop your plan

We will develop your plan by listing tasks, by adding dates to each of them and by getting an understanding of the resources you will need (Step 7). When your plan is finished, it will look like a clear list of actions with dates, statuses and other relevant details. Your plan will be the document you use to move forward, track your progress and sometimes revise the way you are approaching your project. It's a very useful document and we will build it so that you can pin it somewhere and look at it regularly to give some structure to your journey. Think of Vicky for a minute and how having a plan could help her focus in the limited slots of time she has to move her enterprise forward.

# Is your plan fixed?

Obviously, as with anything we are working on in this book, your plan is not entirely set in stone. The world around you is constantly changing, so you always need to have some flexibility in everything you do. If you find that some actions become irrelevant or that maybe you'd like to change your approach, you absolutely can change it.

# Changing your plan

If you haven't started taking serious action and you are still defining and planning the journey to your vision, you can change anything you like. You won't have made a major commitment yet, so it's perfectly OK to change your mind. This is one of the reasons why this book is organised the way it is: you get to think first, then take action. The only thing to be careful about is ensuring that your scope, objectives, approach and plan still line up when you make the change.

However, if you want to change something and you have already made a serious investment of time and money, there will be a need to spend some time thinking about the impact of what you want to do. Let's say you've signed off the work to build an extension to your house, the building work has started and you suddenly change your mind about what you want. It wouldn't be impossible to make a change (and if you really made a mistake, you might as well catch yourself early) but you would have to think this through and assess the impact of the change on your vision, your resources and even on your success partners. For example, I wouldn't want my husband to decide to spend all our savings on retraining as a physiotherapist, then change his mind half-way through his training (and several thousand pounds later) and decide that he now wants to be a photographer. Before he commits more money I would request that we spend some time questioning why he wants the change and understanding the pros and cons.

Having said all this, since we are still in the planning phase, I'm assuming you've not progressed with the big actions yet and you can still refine your plan.

# Make it fly

Before developing your plan, I recommend that you review all the work we have done to date to refresh your memory on all aspects of what you want. This is particularly useful if you have taken a break between Steps 5 and 6. Doing this will not only bring all the details back to the fore but also get you in the right sort of mood (hopefully very motivated and excited about your vision!).

The usual drill: make sure you have the time to do the exercise and get hold of what you need.

---

**STEP 6 EXERCISE**

**PRODUCE A DRAFT PLAN**

1. Download the plan template from the website or create your own based on the example below.

2. Get hold of your approach and, for each objective or goal, ask yourself "What do I need to do to get there?". Then detail the steps you will take and the date you will perform each of them. If you are unsure how long a particular step will take, just put in an estimate. For example, you may not know how long it will take you to find a gym you like in your area, but you can guess that a month

---

is probably enough as you are unlikely to want to visit more than three gyms.

3. When you are done, read the whole plan and imagine that you are performing the actions. As you do so, ask yourself whether the order of the actions is logical and whether the dates you have set are realistic. For example, you may not be able to work out how to fund some building work until you've been given an estimate, and you may not have an estimate until you have found a builder. This is called having "dependencies" – when one task is dependent on another.

4. Write down your key assumptions, observations, etc. to go with your plan. Make sure you note everything that springs to mind: this will be important later.

A draft plan for the project "change your lifestyle and live longer" is given overleaf.

We can note some key assumptions and observations about the plan:

- Although at this stage it seems feasible to complete all the week 1 activities in the same week, it may be a little ambitious. This client needs to think about what else is going on in her life and make sure she can realistically complete all that she has committed to in the plan. This is why she has slipped "purchase books on meditation" to week 3.

- She had not included any activities to review her progress on a regular basis. This is because we will set up a way to review progress in Part 4.

| Tasks / Actions | Month 1 | | | | Month 2 | | | |
|---|---|---|---|---|---|---|---|---|
| | WK1 | WK2 | WK3 | WK4 | WK5 | WK6 | WK7 | WK8 |
| **Lose 1 Stone** | | | | | | | | |
| Investigate slimming clubs | ■ | | | | | | | |
| Join | | ■ | | | | | | |
| Follow programme (lose 2lb per week) | | | ■ | ■ | ■ | ■ | ■ | ■ |
| **Tone & Strengthen Body** | | | | | | | | |
| Investigate gyms in my area | ■ | | | | | | | |
| Visit to assess facility | | ■ | | | | | | |
| Choose the best gym for me & join | | ■ | | | | | | |
| Organise session to have programme developed | | ■ | | | | | | |
| Attend session | | | ■ | | | | | |
| Follow programme | | | | ■ | ■ | ■ | ■ | ■ |
| **Reduce Stress by 50%** | | | | | | | | |
| Plan breaks into my work calendar every day | ■ | | | | | | | |
| Start taking breaks | | ■ | | | | | | |
| Take breaks every day | | | ■ | ■ | ■ | ■ | ■ | ■ |
| Plan leaving on time into my work calendar | ■ | | | | | | | |
| Start leaving on time | | ■ | | | | | | |
| Leave on time every day | | | ■ | ■ | ■ | ■ | ■ | ■ |
| Purchase books on meditation | | | ■ | | | | | |
| Read books | | | | ■ | | | | |
| Meditate | | | | ■ | ■ | ■ | ■ | ■ |

| Month 3 | | | | Month 4 | | | | Month 5 | | | |
|---|---|---|---|---|---|---|---|---|---|---|---|
| WK9 | WK10 | WK11 | WK12 | WK13 | WK14 | WK15 | WK16 | WK17 | WK18 | WK19 | WK20 |
| | | | | | | | | | | | |
| | | | | | | | | | | | |
| | | | | | | | | | | | |
| | | | | | | | | | | | |
| | | | | | | | | | | | |
| | | | | | | | | | | | |
| | | | | | | | | | | | |
| | | | | | | | | | | | |
| | | | | | | | | | | | |
| | | | | | | | | | | | |

# Step 7

## Make sure you have what you need

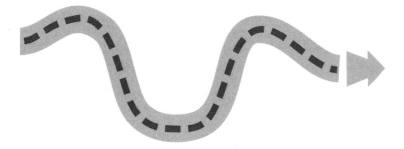

*"The greatest achievement of the human spirit is to live up to one's opportunities and make the most of one's resources."*

Vauvenargues

As you were building your plan, you may have realised that some activities will need to involve other people. If what you want is quite simple, as in the "changing lifestyle" example, it may be that all the actions are yours. However, let's say your end goal involves adding an extension to your house. It is entirely possible that you are able to do all the building work yourself, but it is more likely that you will need to hire a professional builder or even a variety of different contractors. This means that in order for your plan to be complete, you will need to include the activities of other people. In this case, these people will be known as "resources".

# Using external resources

In addition to adding the activities to your plan, you will also have to make sure that the builder's proposal and their estimates are sensible (that their work is appropriately defined). The skills you have learnt in Step 1 will come in handy to ensure that the quote the builder gives you is an accurate "scope" of work for the piece they will deliver. It needs to include a list of deliverables and key dates as well as an overall cost. The contract with your builder may also specify what happens if they overrun, particularly if they find that their initial assessment was incorrect and they need to take more time to deliver and to charge you more. Is the price fixed or will it increase if it takes more time? (I'm not an expert on building work, so if this is your project, make sure you get any quote or estimate reviewed by a professional.)

# Managing other people and risks

Managing other people is an art, so is being able to keep projects to scope, plan and budget. The key is for the work to be as clearly defined and as comprehensive as possible before you start and sign the contract. On top of that and because it's not possible to control everything, I would also recommend that you spend time thinking through everything that could possibly go wrong and to assess the impact of the worst-case scenario. This is called "assessing the risks". We will discuss managing risks and issues in Part 3, but as you build your plan I would like you to start thinking of the possibility of something going wrong, particularly when you need to engage the services of third parties and when scarce resources are involved (e.g. money). If you are adept at positive thinking, this may feel alien. "How can I think about what might go wrong? You said our thoughts create our world ...". Yes, that's right, but however positive you are, there are risks and there are unknowns. The great thing about risks is that they may never materialise. So, do not "plan" for them to happen, just think "what if" and take some precautions. You can then use positive thinking to keep the risks at bay!

## The excitement of a new thing

Most third parties will not willingly set out to deceive you; however, because this may be the first time they hear about your vision, they may not be as clear about it as you are, which could lead to the wrong plan (and cost). Because you know what you want so well and you are passionate about it, you may miss some very important information (particularly the aspects you like less). In addition, when you first contract with someone, you are likely to get truly excited about seeing your vision coming together and you may be less cautious than you should be. This is normal. Lastly, you may feel confident in your third party because they have performed work for you before. Although this is great, it's not a guarantee that they have clearly understood what you want.

Irrespective of the circumstances, irrespective of how positive things feel, you must park your excitement and enlist your rational mind to think about the possibility that things may go wrong. Here's a real-life example to illustrate the importance of assessing your risks and providing some contingency.

## Things do go wrong at times, however much you plan; the trick is to be able to recover

Tom and Paula had been working on renovating their house for a while and the previous year had modernised their bathroom. The workmanship was of very high quality and they were very happy with the result. Their house was from the Victorian era and, as is typical in England, the previous owners had built an extension at the back. The bathroom was on the top floor of this extension, and on the ground floor there was a kitchen. The couple's next plan was to renovate their kitchen. They had been talking about this to the contractor who fitted their bathroom and he had recommended a builder from his network who he promised would work to the same level of quality. Tom and Paula felt very confident, particularly after they met the builder and got a quote. They didn't think anything could go wrong. They just got really excited.

Unfortunately, three days into the job, the builder discovered that the extension had been built without any foundation. The builder made Tom and Paula aware there was a high risk that the extension could start sinking into the ground, which would damage not only the kitchen but also the new bathroom. It was up to them: they could take the risk or they could turn the project into a much bigger one by ensuring a new foundation was built. All of a sudden, the time quoted went up by a month and the price by 50%.

Tom and Paula were in shock. They had not anticipated this situation and had spent their entire budget on the modernisation of the kitchen. They had not thought of keeping some money in reserve just in case. In the end, the couple decided to build the foundation and to take out a loan to cover the extra cost. This wasn't ideal but at least it meant that what they had invested in their bathroom and were investing in their kitchen would be protected, as well, of course, as their overall investment in their house.

For all the third parties you add to your plan and even for your own actions, start getting into the habit of asking yourself, "what if?" and if there is a cost to what you are doing, put 20% aside to cover eventualities. If you can identify a big risk, like the one in the Tom and Paula story, then put even more money aside and wait until you can afford to do the work and have some provision or be conscious that you may have to take out a loan.

# Other types of resources

As well as third parties to complete activities on your plan, you may need other resources. These resources may not be people. If you think of the lifestyle example, a "gym" or a "slimming club" is a resource. Changing careers may involve retraining and finding the right college and course. Resources are all the things you need that will help you get what you want: they can be people, books, courses or, as we've seen, time and money.

You may also need professional or specialist advice. For example, if you want to start your own business, you may need an accountant, a banker and specialist marketing and sales advice. Please use this step to identify all the professional resources or "how to" books you need.

# The importance of looking after your resources

Resources are sometimes limited. If you are like most people I know, you won't have tons of time and money at your disposal. It is therefore important that you put your valuable resources in the right place by spending your time and money on the things that will get you closer to your vision. Putting the effort in and thinking through how you will approach your project, as well as pulling a clear plan together *before* you take action, will help you make the most of your resources.

It is obviously possible that you make a mistake, take the wrong turn and waste some of your resources. Having a clear plan and structure around your vision may not prevent this from happening; however, it is likely that if you follow the method in this book, you will catch yourself before it's too late. If you don't have any structure to get what you want and you don't regularly review your progress and check how close you are to your goals, it may take a lot longer before you realise that what you're doing is actually taking you down the wrong path and that, at the same time, you've also run out of money.

# Make it fly

Let's get you moving with an exercise.

STEP 7 EXERCISE

MAKE SURE YOU HAVE ALL THAT
YOU NEED

1. Pull out your plan.
2. Add a column between Tasks and the first month and call it "Resources".

3. For each task where you either need someone else to complete the work or need access to a resource, include that resource in the Resources box. Feel free to enter your name if the task is to be carried out by you, or just leave the box blank.

4. If you need to chat to professional resources or learn some new skills, add this in as a separate task on the plan.

5. Ensure that you have listed the tasks to identify or engage with your resources.

6. Have a look at the worked examples on the website if you need to.

7. If you have started to identify some risks and issues, make a note of them and we will list them formally in Step 11 when we start pulling our challenges log together.

# Step 8

## Finalise your plan

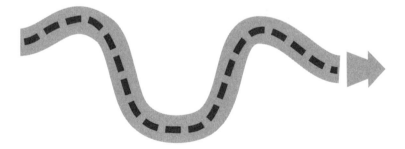

*"Good plans shape good decisions. That's why good planning helps to make elusive dreams come true."*
Lester Robert Bittel

MAKE IT FLY!

Step 8 is about ensuring that your plan is complete, that it has:

- Key activities broken down into tasks. It must also show that you are clear on the deliverables (what you will see or get once you've completed the tasks and activities, for example a book or a new kitchen)
- A status for each activity and task, particularly if you have already started
- A clear list of resources and an estimate of the work that will need to be completed, with a plan on how you will firm up the estimate
- A draft list of risks and issues (for now, please just keep a note of these)
- An estimate of how long each task and activity will take to perform (and if relevant how much they will cost – you should maintain costs in a separate budget sheet)
- An understanding of how tasks and activities interrelate (known as "dependencies") and which tasks and activities are critical to meeting the overall timeframes (the "critical path").

# Your plan will help track progress

Having dates on your plan will help you track progress and address any slippages as soon as they occur. I will encourage you in the "Do it!" box (starting at the end of this step) to refer back to your plan on a regular basis. How well are tasks progressing? Which ones are in progress, which ones are complete? What are you meant to be doing now? How are your external resources performing? Are they on track? Are you on track with your tasks? If either you or your resources are not meeting deadlines, why is this? What is the impact? What are you going to do about it? Are you at risk of losing money?

Learning to bring your plan to life, regularly updating it and improving it is one way to address issues quickly and efficiently but also to keep you motivated. Think about it. Won't it feel good when you set a task to "complete"? Won't it feel good when you are clear about a set of activities a third party needs to perform and you have a mechanism to track them? Won't it feel good when you can see that things are going well or you can figure out why they aren't going so well and are in a position to quickly do something about it?

# The art of estimating

If you are new at estimating and you don't entirely trust the amount of time you have set against particular tasks and activities, take the safe route and give yourself more time. You are better off overestimating than underestimating. Of course, overestimating wildly may not be wise as it may kill your motivation or, if a task is chargeable, render it unaffordable. If you are finding estimating difficult, ask yourself what would help. Is the issue that the task is to be performed by someone else? In which case, get in touch with them and get them to estimate. Maybe it's because you have some research to do in order to clarify the steps? In that case, just put in an estimate, add an activity to conduct the research and then get on with it. Then update your plan with more accurate timings and steps once you are clear. If you don't want to conduct the research now or it doesn't make sense to do so, then estimate and add a percentage of time proportionate to how confident you feel. So if you don't feel confident at all, maybe extend the time by 30%, and if you feel quite confident, only add an extra 10%. You can adjust the time later.

# Dependencies and the critical path to your vision

There are a couple more things to consider when reviewing your plan: dependencies and the critical path to your vision. The dependencies are the tasks which are interrelated, where one of the tasks is dependent on the other. Let's take an example where you want to sell your writing skills. You would not be able to advertise your services until you have defined what you are offering and priced it. Well, I guess you could offer an unclear service, but this is unlikely to attract clients because they wouldn't understand what you mean by a "writing service". What type of writing service? Writing blogs? Editing? Writing business reports? What we can therefore say is that the task "Offer Writing Service" is dependent on the task "Define Writing Service", so if it's going to take you a week to define the service, you have to delay the start of the offering piece by a week. You cannot start both tasks at the same time.

In the above example, we can also say that the task of defining the service is a *critical task* because, as explained, you cannot start offering the service until the task of defining the service has completed, so if that slips by a month, the entire project will slip by a month. This is what is known as the critical path: when a series of tasks are so critical that slippage will impact the overall plan.

By the way, this is only important to help you get the tasks in the right order!

# Make it fly

Let's put this into practice and finalise your plan; make sure you have the time and the tools that you need.

---

**STEP 8 EXERCISE**

**FINALISE YOUR PLAN**

1. Get hold of your plan and review your estimates. Adjust the dates if you need to.

2. Go through all activities and tasks and identify the dependencies. Link the tasks with dependencies with an arrow (to show that something must happen before something else). If you need to, have a look at the worked examples on the website to see a visual representation.

3. For the critical path, just take a look at the path formed by the arrows. It will not be possible to start a task that follows an arrow until the task before the arrow has completed.

---

Starting with this step, I will include a "Do it!" section to remind you to start putting your plan into action. Of course, your plan is not perfect yet (for example, you may still have some research to do) but there are likely to be some steps you can start taking to move towards your vision.

# DO IT!

1. Get hold of your plan and decide what tasks you will complete and by when. These could be the areas where you have some research to do.

2. Build some time in your week to complete those tasks. Make appointments in your diary, then pin your plan on the wall so that you know exactly what to do when your appointment comes up.

3. Build some time each morning and/or evening to sit in silence and visualise what you want (see the exercise in Step 3). This can be done before you get out of bed and/or before you go to sleep.

# Step 9

# Identify your success partners

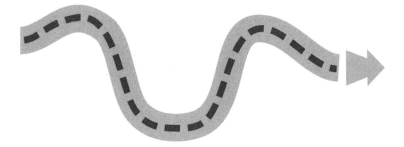

"If everyone is moving forward together, then success takes care of itself."

Henry Ford

Hopefully, moving your vision forward will be a lot of fun and very rewarding, particularly now that you have a clear plan. However, we have to be realistic and consider that at times there will be challenges and you will have to keep yourself upbeat. It would therefore be great to get as much support as you can from the people who matter to you. Having your friends and family on your side as you work on your project will provide you with encouragement when things don't go as well as they could, and someone to celebrate with when they do. Who knows, you may even get some valuable feedback and your success partners may even take it upon themselves to keep you accountable!

There are a couple of questions to ask yourself when it comes to success partners: have you done enough to get their support and are they truly on your side?

# Is everyone on board?

You may be wondering why the people who love you wouldn't be on your side; after all, working to get what you want in life is an exciting and positive activity. It's good for you. Well, this may be the case when you consider your life from your own standpoint, but other people are likely to have different perspectives and priorities, and your project may not be one of them. So what can you do to get their support?

*Tell them how important what you want is to you and get them to feel your passion.* Your vision is real to you, but at the beginning it will be very much inside your head (or hopefully, having done the exercises, on pieces of paper in your workbook). Other people do not have access to your internal world and you can only get them to see what you see by explaining clearly to them how much you want this and by communicating your vision and progress on a regular basis.

Let's say you feel that talking about yourself isn't right or that you're boring people with your stuff, or maybe even that you're embarrassed to have such big dreams. If the people around you do not know enough about your plans or if you downplay their importance, they may be confused. Your potential success partners may therefore be lukewarm about the idea and give you little support. This may not be an issue in the case of a friend but it may be a serious issue in the case of your life partner or your parents, as I'm sure you will be keen on them being more than mildly supportive. In Step 4, we looked at telling the world. Hopefully you will have done so;

however, if you now have more clarity, make sure you keep your success partners in the loop.

*Find out if they find your vision threatening and reassure them.* The people around you may care as much as you do about what you want but in a negative way. They may have a vested interest in you failing to reach your goals because they find your vision scary. They may not be conscious of any of this. For example, let's say you want to change career and there is a risk that you will earn a lot less initially. Your life partner may feel threatened by this. They may be thinking that their lifestyle will have to change and this may not be something they are prepared to do. So they may unconsciously put some obstacles in your way. In this case, not only will you get no support, you will also have to deal with their resistance. This can be depressing when the going gets tough.

In reality, if you communicate well, you'll probably end up with some naturally supportive people and some where you have to do a little bit of work. All I'm asking you to do is to give this aspect some thought and be prepared to take action if you need to. Things are much harder to achieve and more stressful when we insist on going it alone. Being able to ask for help and support can make the journey easier.

# Make it fly

In this section, we'll do some work to find out how the people around you feel about your vision and your project, whether they know too little and are not being given the opportunity to support you fully, or whether they feel threatened by your plans and are about to put some obstacles in your way (either consciously or unconsciously). We will brainstorm the techniques you could use to get as much support as possible. If during the exercise you find people whom you know will not be supportive whatever you do, then at least you will understand their concerns and be in a position to decide what you share and don't share with them.

Now, let's put some of this into practice. Make sure you have the time and tools you need for the exercise.

## STEP 9 EXERCISE

## GETTING SUPPORT

1. Think about all the people who are close to you and list them.

2. Think about all the people who are not close to you personally but who may matter in the context of your vision; for example, the ladies in your evening class may not be that close to you but they could be a good group to use to test some of your ideas.

3. Once you have made a comprehensive list of people, complete the success partner template (available from the website) or answer the following questions for each success partner:

   - What level of power do they hold over you and your vision?

   - What is their attitude towards your vision? Are they for or against?

   - What are their areas of interest?

   - What are their areas of resistance?

   - What do you want from them?

   - What do they want from you?

   - How do you plan to engage them? What can you do about their resistance?

   - How will you keep them engaged?

4. If doing this has led to some actions, update your plan with your "success partner tasks".

## DO IT!

1. Get hold of your plan and review the tasks you have progressed according to what you set out to do in the previous step. If you have completed some tasks, change their status to

complete. If some have slipped, assess the impact and decide what you need to do, then adjust your plan.

2. Decide what tasks you will complete next and build some time in your week to complete those tasks. Make appointments in your diary.

3. Build some time each morning and/or evening to sit in silence and visualise getting what you want (see the exercise in Step 3).

PART **3**
GET OUT OF
YOUR OWN WAY

# PART 3

# Get out of your own way

*"What is necessary to change a person is to change his awareness of himself."*
Abraham Maslow

Congratulations! You have reached a key stage on the way to your vision. By now (provided you have completed the exercises), what you want will be much clearer, you will have defined your approach and formulated a clear action plan, and you will have started to build some support around you.

Cast your mind back to the Introduction. I said this book was different because it addressed both the logical and the emotional sides of making things happen. What I have noticed is that in the world of work the logical approach is preferred, but in the world of personal development it's the opposite: the emotional tends to be the focus. I'm offering you a method that includes both because you will need both: the logical steps of defining and planning will help you take action, and the emotional steps will help you stay motivated, increase your confidence and make you more resilient when the road to your vision gets bumpy.

Apart from the vision exercises, we have not spent much time yet dealing with anything emotional, although because you can't separate the two, some feelings and beliefs will have cropped up and your intuition may be starting to tell you about the challenges you will face.

As you work through this section, bear in mind that, although all the steps are important, you can have the greatest impact on your desires through action you take in this part of the book. The power to get what you want in life lies within you. You are the one who decides to complete the tasks on your plan, to do something about challenges and to ask for help when you need it. Without your drive to make things happen, your project doesn't exist. Changing how you view your world may be the one thing that makes all the difference.

Before we get started, I would like you to promise to be gentle and patient with yourself. Our world often encourages quick solutions but I would like you to adopt a different mindset as you work with personal challenges. Changing beliefs and behaviours, facing up to your fears and building your self-confidence could shift in an instant or take months or years. Often, there's also a need for repetition and a willingness to try different techniques until you find the one that works for you. Sometimes you won't even know which one worked, just that you've changed. Entire books have been written about the topics we will cover. Since we have limited space, my aim is to help you become aware of what may stop you getting what you want, to give you some tools to get you started, but also to provide you with some references so that you can go into more depth if you need to.

# Step 10

## Look after YOU

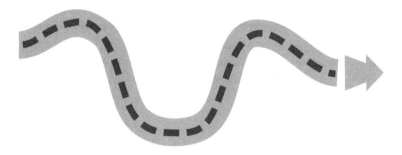

*"The higher your energy level, the more efficient your body, the better you feel and the more you will use your talent to produce outstanding results."*
Tony Robbins

Looking after yourself is a vital part of making things happen. We said that your project doesn't exist outside you, that you are what brings energy to your vision. It is therefore really important that you keep your energy high and positive, both physically and mentally. In this step, we will explore different ways you can look after yourself. My goal is to help you decide where to focus, then to build on your success, rather than to get everything right first time. You may need more than one attempt before you are able to balance work, family and friends with the need to exercise regularly, eat the right food and relax. What we want to achieve in this step is to make you feel better, not to add to your stress! I encourage you to listen to your intuition. Maybe what you resist the most is what would make the most difference? Or maybe lots of little changes across all areas will work best for you?

# Why looking after yourself matters

When you feel good, life flows better, you have the energy you need to move forward and you can handle challenges from a solid foundation. You are calm and positive, so you make good decisions. You don't feel stressed, so you take time to brainstorm and be creative. If something is hurting or if you're feeling tired or frustrated, this state is likely to influence what you decide and whether you move forward. Anger, stress and pain can often cause us to make rash and emotional decisions. You don't want to end up dismissing something that could have made a real difference to your dream, just because you're not feeling quite yourself.

When you feel good, people are also drawn to you and, depending on your aspirations, this may be very important. Think of a time when you met someone who was down, frustrated or stressed. What impact did they have on you and your energy? If they were just passing in your life and you were feeling good yourself, probably not much impact. If, however, they were trying to sell you something or engage you in some activity, it is likely that your energy dipped when they got in contact with you. Picture an angry, aggressive salesman trying to sell you a car. How likely are you to buy? Or even a stressed-out personal trainer – how likely are you to enjoy your workout? How we feel impacts our own energy but also that of others and in turn how they behave towards us.

Lastly, how much you care for yourself sometimes reflects how much you love yourself. This is not an easy thing to admit, but often we treat others better than we do ourselves. Think of your internal voice. Is it kind and caring? Does it talk to you the way you would talk to other people? The central message in author Louise Hay's work is self-love. Try Louise's mirror test. Look at yourself in the mirror. Make sure you look directly into your own eyes. Then tell yourself how much you love yourself and you appreciate being you. This seems simple, doesn't it? Try it and see what happens. To take care of yourself well, you have to love yourself.

# Take care of your body

Taking care of your body is essential to feel good physically and have the energy to get things done. This means, at the very least, eating well, exercising and resting. How well are you doing in each area?

Do you eat healthy nutritious food? It used to be that if you ate a balanced diet with lots of fruit and vegetables and a moderate amount of proteins and carbohydrate, you stood a good chance of being able to answer "yes" to this question. However, nowadays you also have to ensure that the food you eat has not been overly processed or hasn't lost all its goodness from being in storage or transported for too long. Think of fruit imported from a faraway location compared with food grown in your back garden. A good rule of thumb is to eat food that is as fresh as possible, comes from somewhere local and is free from pesticides. Ian Marber (The Food Doctor) and Patrick Holford (the Institute for Optimum Nutrition) have published several books on nutrition if you are interested in finding out more on the basic principles, or even how you can use food to cure ailments and affect your mood.

Do you exercise regularly? Exercise not only helps to keep you fit and flexible, it also improves how you feel and keeps stress at bay. As a result of physical activity, your body releases feel-good hormones called endorphins, and the fact that you have to concentrate on what you're doing (otherwise you may fall off your bike!) causes your focus to shift away from problems and worries. You end up feeling happier and less stressed as a result. In the old days, exercise was part and parcel of our lives and many occupations were physical. In modern society, many occupations involve sitting down for long periods of time. If this is the case for you, ensuring you exercise regularly will be important, particularly as you get older and your bones and muscles need regular movement to keep working well.

Do you take time to recharge your batteries? Sleep and rest are essential to replenish our energy. As adults, we need between seven and eight and a half hours of uninterrupted sleep at night. And this has to be good-quality sleep where you get up feeling rested and full of energy. Lack of sleep can make us irritable and unable to cope. In serious cases, it can even cause anxiety and depression and affect our brain functions. If you have trouble sleeping, a good wind-down routine may help. This could be having a warm bath, listening to relaxing music or doing some breathing exercises. What you are trying to do is to switch off from the day as well as tell your mind and body that it's time for sleep. I like to read something inspiring before I get to sleep. I normally end up dropping off naturally as well as going to sleep with positive thoughts in my mind. If you consider that your last thought stays with you for the first four hours of the night, making it an inspiring one is not a bad idea.

If you need some more help developing good habits, there's a nice book by John Whiteman called *9 Days to Feel Fantastic*. John's method is simple but what it does well is encourage you to make changes to your everyday life by adopting one new habit every day.

# Take care of your mind

There is a strong connection between the mind and the body and some of the areas we looked at previously will also impact how you feel mentally. For example, exercise can help with depression and moods (remember the feel-good hormones), nutrition can give the right fuel to the brain, and sleep can affect your ability to concentrate. In this section, we will look at some additional things you could do to stay positive.

Be very careful what you feed your mind. Constant exposure to negative information and people is simply not good for you. Of course, if you maintain a healthy mind, negativity will have less impact, but without wanting to try the experiment, I would say that constant exposure to depressing news, angry people or criticism will eventually grind you down. So why risk it? Put all the chances on your side and avoid as much negative exposure as you can. A study[1] by James Fowler and Nicholas Christakis conducted over 20 years demonstrated that people's happiness was affected by the happiness of other people with whom they were connected through their

---

1 Fowler, J.H. and Christakis, N.A. 'Dynamic spread of happiness in a large social network; longitudinal analysis over 20 years in the Framingham Heart Study', *British Medical Journal*, 2008, 337, a2, 338, 1–9

social network. Other studies have also shown that emotions are contagious and that if at university you were assigned a depressed roommate, you would become depressed yourself over time.

Learn to relax your mind and to create space for creative thoughts. If your mind is constantly churning, not only will it get tired, it will block new information. Einstein said that the definition of insanity was doing the same things over and over again and expecting different results. If there is no space for new thoughts in the incessant chatter of your mind, it will be difficult to get the perspective you need to think differently. Let's say you're worried about a speech you're giving at work the next day. You're trying to prepare but the worry takes over and your mind seems to go into an endless spin of unhelpful thoughts preventing you from calmly assessing the situation and finding ways to handle the challenges. The trick is to stop your mind from spinning and to relax, but how can you do that when you're stressed? On the spur of the moment, you could try using a relaxation technique, for example a deep-breathing exercise (see below). However, for longer-term benefits, meditation is something worth investigating.

Meditation works by helping you focus on the present moment. The theory is that you can't change the past and you can't control the future, so thinking about either leads to stress. Excessive thinking about past events creates resentment, guilt or shame, whilst a focus on the future causes worry and anxiety. Meditation teaches how to control your mind and your thoughts by bringing them back to the present moment. When you become good at this, you can catch your mind before it goes into unhelpful thinking patterns and stop the stress from escalating (it's easier to reduce stress if you can catch it early than once it's gone into overdrive).

Although meditation is often associated with eastern philosophy and religion, it has grown in popularity in the West as a technique for reducing stress and anxiety, improving focus and even strengthening the immune system. Think about it as relaxation for your mind and as a way to focus your thinking where you can have impact rather than on the stuff you can't change. There are lots of courses and resources on meditation but for a less spiritual, more practical and fun way of getting into it, try www.getsomeheadspace.com.

## SIMPLE BREATHING EXERCISE

Try the following to relax your mind. Find a place where you won't be disturbed and sit down with your back against the chair and your feet flat on the floor (don't lie down – you may go to sleep). Close your eyes and focus on your breath: in, out, in, out. You can say the words "in", "out", "in", "out". Each time a thought comes into your mind, acknowledge it but let it pass and come back to your breath, in, out, in, out. Do this for 10 minutes. Don't check the clock; put a timer on if you need to. Do your breathing exercise before your visualisation exercise in the morning and in the evening to relax and clear your mind. Or, use your breathing exercise when something happens that knocks you off balance, stresses you or makes you angry. Just sit still, close your eyes and breathe.

I find that if I focus on my breath for more than five minutes, I go to sleep. I've tried on my own, in a group (that was embarrassing!) and with a CD. No matter where I am or the time of day, if there is no sound, I sleep. However, I have discovered that if I listen to relaxing music at the same time, I'm fine. If this happens to you too, try listening to something like Dr Wayne Dyer and James F. Twyman's 'I Am Wishes Fulfilled Meditation' CD. The sounds have a deep relaxing effect, and somehow listening to music helps me stay awake.

# Be grateful and stay positive

A calm mind in a fit and healthy body will go a long way to help you feel good and positive about your life and about your desires. Before we move on, I'd like to give you two simple but powerful techniques we haven't discussed yet: keeping a gratitude journal and staying optimistic by using positive affirmations.

Do you give thanks for the good things in your life? Robert Emmons (University of California, Davis) and his colleagues conducted a study where they asked a group of people to keep a gratitude journal for two months. Each week, they had to note in their journal five simple things like someone being kind to them, a warm summer day or learning something new. They asked a second group of people to note their weekly hassles in their journal and a third group to record neutral life events. At the end of the two months, there were significant positive results in the gratitude group. Participants stated that they were feeling better overall, were more optimistic about the future, and reported fewer health problems and a better quality of sleep. The researchers also observed that those in the gratitude group were more likely to have made progress on personal goals (this is important to us!). Subsequent research demonstrated that keeping a daily journal had even more impact.

When it comes to optimism, Martin Seligman, one of the founders of positive psychology, discovered that optimists stand more chances of getting what they want in life because they persist where pessimists give up. Through his research, Seligman found that this is because optimists assign failure to something external, which often they have the power to change. For example, if they fail to make a sale, they will rationalise that the attitude of the customer is to blame. They may tell themselves things like "the customer was in a bad mood" or "the customer had no need for my product". This suggests that if they come across the right customer, they will sell. All they have to do is find those customers. Pessimists, on the other hand, attribute the failure to themselves or to something they can't change. They tell themselves things like "I didn't sell because I'm no good" or "nobody wants to buy from me". It is much harder to persist if you think the issue is a flaw in your character. Interestingly, the main difference between the optimists and the pessimists in our example isn't skills and experience, it is the little voice inside their heads.

You can increase optimism by using positive affirmations. A positive affirmation is a short present-tense statement where you tell yourself something good to lessen a negative belief, for example "I love going to the gym", "I'm good at selling" or "I find people who want my product". It doesn't matter if you believe the statement at first; the idea is that if you keep repeating it, it will impact your subconscious. Think about the alternative for a minute. Is telling yourself that you hate the gym or that you're rubbish at selling likely to help more?

I find that a good way to use these techniques is to try to turn them into daily habits. I stuck my affirmations about my goals on the walls next to my bathroom mirror and behind my computer so that I can see them every time I walk past. I also have them on the notepad in my phone so that I can refer to them when I travel (this is useful if I need extra motivation on my way to, let's say, a difficult meeting). I also have a wind-down routine before bed. Not only does writing in your journal and visualising encourage positive thoughts, as I said before, it also puts you in a good frame of mind for sleep. And yes, I sometimes forget to do my affirmations and to wind down before I get to bed. The pieces of paper are a good way to remind me the next day.

# Take care of your environment

Does the environment you live in support you? When you look at your surroundings, do you feel good? By environment, I mean both your home but also the area you live in. If your house is in desperate need of repair or you don't feel safe where you live, you are unlikely to feel good. In fact, you are likely to feel stressed, uncomfortable and insecure. Clearly, feeling like this will affect your energy.

Potentially, you may not be in a position to move or repair your home. This may actually be your vision. If that is the case, what I'm asking you to do is to become aware of the impact of your environment and to brainstorm what you could do to improve things until you find a way to a more permanent solution. Maybe there are some small repairs you could do now? Maybe you could paint a room a brighter colour whilst you wait for the money to refurbish it more thoroughly? Maybe you could regularly escape from your environment by taking the train to the opposite end of the city where there are nice parks or nature areas? Maybe you could take a trip to the country on your day off? Some of these don't cost much and they will make a difference to your state of mind and your wellbeing. Extracting yourself from your environment will also help you see new possibilities by breaking out of your routine.

Create space for what you want to come into your life; get rid of anything you don't use or want. There is a principle that says if your house or your life is full, there will be no space for new things. Don't take a chance with this one, just do it. This is your cue to de-clutter! Go through your wardrobe and cupboards. Get rid of any food that's passed its sell-by date. Give any clothes you haven't worn for a year to charity. Clear your filing cabinet of old papers you don't need to keep. Clear out your loft, your garage or any other area you use as a dumping ground. I promise you'll feel really good afterwards and you may even get some exercise as an added bonus!

# Take care of your resources

We talked about protecting your resources in the planning step. We discussed the importance of evaluating risks and setting some resources aside to cover them. The example I used was having enough money to complete a building job. Here, I would like to discuss a couple more things: how to make sure you make the most of your resources and the need to create reserves.

It is likely that to get what you want you will need time or money or maybe both. You'll need time to complete the tasks on your plan and you may need money to fund some of the activities. As both time and money are finite resources, we need to make sure that the need for them doesn't cause you any additional stress or fear. We will do this by ensuring that you start from a position of strength, i.e. a position where you have some time and some money to spare.

Cast your mind back to Vicky. I know that the key issue was that she didn't have a written plan; however, another challenge for her was that with three young children, her time was at a premium. Luckily, she did have some time on Thursday mornings. What do you think would have happened if she didn't have any time at all? It is likely that the pressures of her dream would have caused her stress and maybe even fear and would have seriously impacted her ability to move forward.

# Money

How well are you doing with money? If you don't need any money to get what you want, I would still advise you to look at this area because money issues will affect your sense of wellbeing. Marie-Claire Carlyle, author of the book *Money Magnet Mindset*, believes that the one thing that affects our ability to attract more money in our lives is our mind. According to Marie-Claire, it comes down to how much we think we deserve to keep.

Look at your current situation. How does what you earn compare with what you spend? Do you spend everything you earn? Or are you good at saving some money each month? Or do you spend more than you earn? Be honest. If you need some money for your dream, the first thing to do is to get yourself on an even keel; then, and only then, can you consider how you will fund your dream. If money is an issue for you, I would encourage you to explore the topic further by getting hold of Marie-Claire's book.

What you want is a situation where you have a healthy attitude to money so that it is not a cause of stress for you.

# Time

What about time? How well are you doing in this area? Most of us lead busy lives where there is a big call on our time. Balancing family, work and friends and still finding time for exercise and to work on your project can be difficult. Do you have enough time to dedicate to your project? If you need to create some more time, you could review everything you do and ask yourself whether you could stop doing it (e.g. watching a particular TV programme) or could delegate it. If you have the money, could you hire someone to help with the housework or look after the hard jobs in the garden? If you don't have the money, are there people who live with you who could help? If you have children, getting them to help around the house will not only lend you a hand, it will prepare them for later life.

If you have the time and you still find it hard to spend time on your project, maybe formalising the time you spend could help. Try booking sessions in your agenda, booking appointments with the people you need to meet, locking yourself in a room or working somewhere away from the house, for example your local coffee shop. If the issue is that you get distracted, we'll take a look at this in Step 16.

# Make it fly

My aim for this step was to cover each topic enough to raise your awareness of areas that may need some improvement and give you some tools and resources to help you start making changes. Hopefully, you will now have some idea of the changes you'd like to make.

Let's look at how we can practically take forward some of the suggestions. Take out your materials and complete the exercise below.

## STEP 10 EXERCISE

## WELLBEING

As I said earlier, you don't have to do everything that is listed below all at the same time; pick the areas that need the most focus first. Remember to use your intuition.

### Body

1. Make a commitment to get moving for at least 30 minutes three times per week. If you don't like the gym, find something else: go for a power walk around the neighbourhood, join a dance class, take up yoga or karate. Whatever you do, get a good mix of heart pumping and body toning and flexing type activities.

2. Before you eat or drink something, ask yourself: "Will this increase or lower my energy levels?"

3. Build exercise sessions into your plan. If you need to learn more about nutrition or to design a new menu for yourself, add this to your plan.

### Mind

1. Find time to sit still and relax each day. Build this into your daily schedule by booking it in your diary.

2. Decide what you need to do to expose your mind to positive influences. Build this into your plan.

3. Become aware of what you need to let go. Make a list and for each item repeat "I cast the burden of xyz to the wind and I go free." Replace xyz with your issue. Another way to let go is to write down on a piece of paper everything that comes to mind when you think of the thing you need to let go until nothing more comes and you are empty. This works particularly well if you are angry. Then burn the piece of paper, shred it or rip it up. There are plenty of books out there on letting go and forgiving if the advice in this one is not sufficient.

If you have serious issues from the past, it may even be time to look at therapy or counselling.

## Environment

1. Review your environment. What is supporting you and what is draining you? Can you address what is draining you? If not, what could you do for now? Add your actions to your plan.
2. De-clutter!

## Stay positive

1. Start a journal or use your diary to record how you feel every day. Each night, write how well you did at interrupting negative thoughts and chatter, what you've observed, what you've learnt. Finish your writing session by including three things you're grateful for – they could be simple things like the sun shining all day.

## Resources

1. Brainstorm what you could delegate and add actions to your plan to make it so.
2. Add actions to your plan to build reserves so that you can make decisions from a place of strength rather than one of fear.

## DO IT!

1. Get hold of your plan and review the tasks you have progressed according to what you set out to do in the previous step. If you have completed some tasks, change their status to complete. If some have slipped, assess the impact and decide what you need to do, then adjust your plan.
2. Decide what tasks you will complete next and build some time in your week to complete those tasks. Make appointments in your diary.

3. Build some time each morning and/or evening to sit in silence and visualise getting what you want (see the exercise in Step 3).

4. Build some time to look after YOU in your schedule.

# Step 11

## Will you go the whole hog?

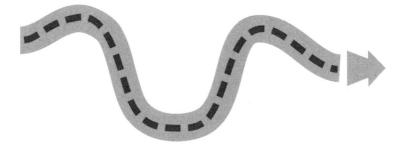

*"If you aren't going all the way, why go at all?"*
Joe Namath

Now that we've made some progress helping you increase your sense of wellbeing, we are ready to look at the challenges you may face as you progress your plans. Remember what we said earlier. You will stand a much better chance of dealing effectively with challenges if you work through them from a place where you feel good about yourself.

You will face two types of challenges: those caused by *you* and those caused by the environment or other people. Both types need to be addressed as soon as you become aware of them. If you ignore issues, they will come back and bite you later. That's a promise.

# Challenges caused by *you*

All human beings face personal challenges, whether in the form of limiting beliefs, fears or weaknesses. These often translate into patterns of behaviours. If you have done some work on yourself, you may know what your challenges are and you may have learnt to turn them into a positive. For example, I'm impatient. This is a challenge if I'm standing in line or if something doesn't work first time around, but it's a great strength when I need to push forward and take action. So if I become frustrated, I try to use my "impatience" to encourage myself to take action. I still get frustrated, but because I can recognise the pattern there is a much better chance that I will do something rather than sit there and stew.

Unfortunately, we are not always aware of our own issues and, more importantly, of the impact they have on the people around us and on our own lives. This is because many of these issues have been relegated to our unconscious. Our hang-ups are often formed when we are made to feel bad about a trait of character, so we decide to hide that trait to feel accepted and loved. Over time, we get used to pushing that trait away and fighting against our own nature. The hidden trait becomes repressed. For example, we may have been loud and boisterous as a child, something that wasn't acceptable to our parents. Maybe we were told something later on in life, when we started work, for example that intuition and feelings were something you left at home. So, we may have chosen to hide those traits and show a more rational and cold persona in the office, losing out on some very good skills in the process. Whatever our life experience, we will have been told by someone, at some point, something that will have affected us negatively. If these experiences were strong enough or repeated over time, they may have led to limiting beliefs, fears or low self-esteem.

It is important to note that you don't need major trauma to end up with limited beliefs. Simply growing up in a family where there is a belief that money is scarce and you have to work hard to get some will have caused you to adopt some beliefs.

# Personal challenges can be bad habits

Personal challenges may also be bad habits picked up along the way. If your parents were worriers, you may have picked up the habit yourself, whether or not you have an anxious disposition. In this case, nobody made you feel bad about yourself; you just learnt to behave a certain way based on the behaviours of those around you. Sometimes, these behaviours can be useful, but sometimes they may be detrimental. If you were "taught" to worry, to be critical of differences or to fear change, it would be good to know, so that if any of these are stopping your progress, you'll be able to do something about them.

# Awareness as a tool

The personal challenges we will look at in this book are the ones you are likely to be able to shift or lessen by becoming aware of them and taking action. However, changing deep-seated beliefs and patterns of behaviour can be tricky, so do not hesitate to look for additional resources if you need to.

# Challenges caused by the outside world

The world and other people may also be the source of challenges. Maybe the venue you've booked for your wedding is flooded a month before the event, maybe your fantastic personal trainer decides to move away half-way through your fitness programme, or maybe your best friend un-consciously tries to stop you working on your vision. As we said in the planning step, no matter how well you plan, no matter how many times you ask yourself "what if?", you will not foresee all the challenges that will come your way. So what should you do? Just as with the personal challenges, the goal is to get you used to identifying issues quickly and acting on them as soon as you can.

# Your challenges log

In this step we will make a start on listing the challenges we may face (risks) and those we are currently facing (issues). It is not that important to get the difference right, as long as you list everything that comes to mind, whether it is likely to happen or has happened already.

You will list your challenges in a log. Just like everything else in this book, it is very important that you write your findings down, firstly so that you end up with a good list, and secondly so that we can do some work to either prevent the problem from occurring or address it. As I said earlier, ignoring issues is, in my view, a key cause of failure. If you find a challenge, you need to do something about it and you need to do something the moment you become aware.

# Make it fly

Let's now think through what risks you may encounter and what issues you currently have. Take out your materials and complete the exercise below.

---

**STEP 11 EXERCISE**

**BUILD A CHALLENGES LOG**

1. Download the Challenges Log template from the website or create your own (there is a table below this exercise listing each column heading in the template).

2. As you were defining or planning your goals, some challenges may have come to mind. If you have made some notes, pull them out, otherwise

---

just spend some time brainstorming by asking yourself what may trip you up along the way. Spend a good amount of time on this and try to make the list as exhaustive as possible.

3. Enter what you find in the challenges log.

4. For each challenge that may occur (the risks), enter ways you could prevent it.

5. For each challenge that has already happened (the issues), enter ways to deal with it.

6. Add some tasks on your plan to ensure that you do something about your challenges.

The table explains how to complete each column of the Challenges Log template. For an example of a completed challenges log, take a look at the worked examples on the website.

| | |
|---|---|
| Number | A number for the challenge. Give each challenge a different one. |
| Description | Describe what has happened or what may happen. |
| What is the impact? | What is or will be the impact of this challenge? |
| What will I do about this? | What are you going to do to resolve this or stop it from happening? |
| How much of a problem is this? | How big is this problem? |
| Status (Open, Closed) | Is this still a problem, is it likely to be a problem, or has it been addressed or gone away? |

# DO IT!

1. Get hold of your plan and review the tasks you have progressed according to what you set out to do in the previous step. If you have completed some tasks, change their status to complete. If some have slipped, adjust your plan.

2. Decide what tasks you will complete next and build some time in your week to complete those tasks as well as to continue working through the book. If you haven't added issues and risks tasks to your plan, review your risks and issues log and plan some tasks around addressing issues and mitigating risks.

3. Build some time each morning and/or evening to sit in silence and visualise reaching your goals (see the exercise in Step 3).

4. Build some time to look after YOU in your schedule.

# Step 12

# The problem with beliefs

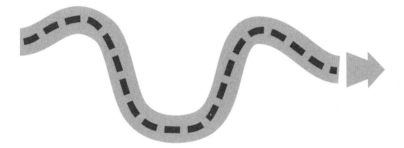

*"Beliefs have the power to create and the power to destroy. Human beings have the awesome ability to take any experience of their lives and create a meaning that disempowers them or one that can literally save their lives."*

Tony Robbins

In Step 11, we briefly discussed how beliefs could be good or detrimental to achieving what you want in life. In this step, we will talk mostly about limiting beliefs, the ones that will stop you from fulfilling your potential and realising your vision. If you come across some positive beliefs as you work through the limiting ones, make a note of them and I'll show you how to complete an "opportunity log" towards the end of this step, so that as well as dealing with your limiting beliefs you can make the most of the "expanding" ones!

# Where do beliefs come from?

Beliefs come from your life experiences; they are formed by what you have observed and what has happened to you. For example, someone brought up in an insecure environment may have grown to believe that other people are out to get them. In that case, they may have difficulty trusting others as they go through life. If, however, someone has been brought up in a secure environment, they may have come to think that everyone is always trying their best to be helpful, so when they go out in the world, they start from a position of trust. Obviously, I'm not saying that everyone is trustworthy; what I'm saying is that unless you get a feeling or a reason not to trust, the natural tendency of someone high in trust would be to expect the best out of people, which will tend to be the experience they will create for themselves.

# What is the impact of beliefs?

Beliefs have a big impact on our lives, and by extension our goals, because they shape our everyday experiences. Let's take the belief we've discussed already: "people are out to get me". If you truly believe this to be the case, you will behave accordingly. When you meet new people, you will be withdrawn and cautious, which will more than likely cause people to also become cautious around you (or even nervous). And whilst they may not actually "get you", they will be unlikely to greet you openly and to be generous and helpful towards you. Your attitude and your belief will therefore cause people to act according to your expectations. If, however, you believe that people are always helpful and you behave in an open and trusting manner, you will find that most people will react in an open, generous and helpful manner towards you. Think about it: would you rather be helpful to someone negative and withdrawn or to someone open and trusting?

# What can you do about beliefs?

Becoming aware of your beliefs is the first step towards dealing with them. Once you are aware how your beliefs support or limit your options, you can start taking action. In this section, we will work to identify your beliefs and their impact. It is also important to realise, as mentioned before, that on top of supporting or limiting what you will aim for, your beliefs also shape your experience. There is therefore an argument for shifting the limiting beliefs and getting control over what you create in your life.

Whilst your beliefs appear to be absolutely true to you, you have to remember that they are a thought and thoughts can be challenged and changed.

Let's take an example where you believe that you are not good enough to get promoted. Sure enough, when you are asked about your ambitions, this always comes out one way or another, so your boss starts to believe you and you don't get promoted. Your colleague is no more nor less talented but believes that they deserve to be promoted and, sure enough, when they are asked about their ambition, state positively what they aim to achieve. They speak confidently about what they want and the boss comes to believe in them. The issue isn't one of talent, it's one of belief. You believe you don't deserve promotion, you even make little jokes and comments about it, so the people around you come to see the world your way. Your colleague, on the other hand, believes that they deserve a promotion, so they influence others in thinking the same.

It is a question of where you put your focus. If you focus on the limiting beliefs, this is what you will notice in life and as a result get more of. Focus on an expanding belief and the opposite will occur. Just like a magnet, you will be attracted to people in a similar state of mind to yours. Change your state of mind, your beliefs, and watch what happens.

# Uncovering your beliefs

What if you don't know what your limiting beliefs are? When a challenge comes up, I don't always put my finger on what is going on straight away. That's because beliefs are unconscious. Here are three techniques I've used in the past.

Let's say that your wish is to get promoted at work. You figure out a plan on how you will do this. Your plan involves discussing development opportunities, making your aims clear and focusing on doing your best work. You start off well, but about a month in, you start getting demotivated and even downright frustrated. You're not sure why, so one night you come home and you decide to pull out a sheet of paper and to write down how you feel. At first you get really angry and the words look like "why is this so hard, why is everyone else getting promoted but me, why can't I just be offered an opportunity?", and on it goes. Then something interesting happens, your frustration seems to run out and you start thinking more positively about your situation. Your boss told you just yesterday that your report was really good; the Human Resources lady came around last week and asked if you wanted to attend some management training. It's not all bad, so why are you so fed up? Suddenly you have an epiphany. You realise that you actually don't believe you deserve to be promoted because somewhere you think you're not that good and if you get a bigger job you'll get found out. The belief is "I'm not good enough". You realise that because of this belief, you're scared of progressing, so you're not really grabbing opportunities. You haven't gone back to Human Resources yet to say you'd be delighted to attend the course. You realise that the frustration comes from wanting your promotion but not being able to push ahead, so being stuck. You decide to do something about your belief and to increase your confidence.

The writing exercise has been good for you, but you decide to investigate your beliefs a bit more and the next day you ask your best friend over for dinner. They've known you since you were little and you know they have your best interests at heart. You explain your challenge to them and ask them to help you explore what may be going on. They are a little nervous at first but you reassure them that you won't get upset, whatever they say. They tell you that as you were growing up, they don't really remember your parents encouraging you. You suddenly have another revelation. Your dad was really unhappy that you didn't follow in his footsteps and was always negative about your choice of career. Could this be where your confidence issues come from? Your friend also says that they've noticed that you often suggest in conversation that you don't think you'll ever get this promotion; it's not a big thing, but you do make little comments and maybe people at work are picking up on this. Oh, that's not good. You decide that you will write some positive affirmations about work, your talents and getting promoted and use them to increase your confidence.

By now, you feel you're really starting to understand what stands between you and your promotion. You decide to do one more thing. You've read in a personal development book that often people who push your buttons do so because they remind you of an issue within yourself. You decide to write about one guy at work you don't like much. You jot down everything that comes to mind and then you realise that the issue is that they are very confident, and when you're around them you feel intimidated. Also, you're a little bit jealous. Again this is down to your belief that "you're not good enough". The reason you don't like them is because deep down you would like to be confident. You really must do something about your belief!

We'll use the techniques in the above example in the "Make it fly" section. If you find that you'd like to do some more in-depth work, I would recommend you get hold of some life coaching books or even hire a life coach. Coaching offers good approaches to find and address limitations.

# Dealing with your limiting beliefs

Once you've identified your limiting beliefs, start challenging them on a regular basis and collating real-life examples to illustrate that they are not true in all circumstances, and write the proof down. Focus on experiences that negate your belief. If you believe "you're not good enough", find examples of where you've done well. In the example in the previous section, you could list times when your boss has complimented you, good comments in your appraisal or when you've dealt with a difficult situation particularly well. Challenging beliefs is a technique that is used to help people with depression and anxiety, so it can be quite powerful.

Another great technique is to act "as if you didn't have the belief" to test its credibility. This will help you with attracting situations that contradict your belief. So if you think everyone's out to get you, start behaving in an open and trusting manner just to see what impact this has. Don't worry if you don't "believe" in what you are doing – it doesn't matter. Just "act" and feel as you would if everyone was helpful.

Use positive affirmations to change your thoughts. The act of repeating something to yourself over and over again affects your subconscious, particularly if you are combining this action with the previous suggestions: you repeat to yourself that the world is full of helpful people, you start noticing the helpful people who come your way. A positive cycle is created and with it a new belief. To continue with this example, every morning tell yourself that you will meet helpful people today and repeat the affirmation each time you feel your resolve weakening. To reinforce the affirmation, imagine how you would feel if it was true. And I repeat: it doesn't matter if you feel like a fraud. Just "act" as if.

# How about positive beliefs?

We've focused very much on the beliefs that may be stopping you. You may, however, have some positive beliefs about yourself that we could use to increase your motivation and confidence. Let's say that you are absolutely convinced that what you want will happen. You get frustrated and there are days when you feel less motivated, but deep down you know that the wedding you're planning is going to be absolutely brilliant. No doubt about it. That's a great belief, one we can use. In the exercise, we'll also note the positive beliefs and list how we can make good use of them.

# Make it fly

Time for an exercise – take out your materials.

---

**STEP 12 EXERCISE**

**IDENTIFY YOUR LIMITING BELIEFS**

1. State what you want in the positive as if you are living it; use your visualisation exercise and see what resistance your subconscious brings up. Be very attentive to the feelings in your body.

2. Note everything that comes up, and you should start seeing some beliefs emerging.

---

3. Use some of the other techniques: ask a good friend, focus on a challenging situation in your life, analyse why someone pushes your buttons, etc.

4. Make a list of all your limiting beliefs and add them to your challenges log. You can add them to an existing issue if they go with one, or you can add them on their own.

5. Treat each belief like an issue and start brainstorming ways you will challenge the belief and break the hold it has on you. What positive affirmations will you create?

6. Brainstorm positive beliefs, the ones that will support you, and add them to your opportunity log. Figure out how you will use them to support yourself and drive you forward.

## DO IT!

1. Get hold of your plan and review the tasks you have progressed according to what you set out to do in the previous step. If you have completed some tasks, change their status to complete. If some have slipped, adjust your plan.

2. Decide what tasks you will complete next and build some time in your week to complete those tasks. If you haven't added actions to deal with challenges to your plan, review your challenges log and plan some tasks around addressing issues and mitigating risks. Make sure you add actions to deal with your limiting beliefs. Maybe write your affirmations down on cards and post them around your house.

3. Build some time each morning and/or evening to sit in silence and visualise what you want (see the exercise in Step 3).

4. Build some time to look after YOU in your schedule.

# Step 13

## Deal with fear and sabotage

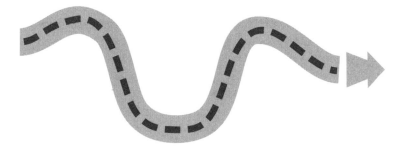

*"We gain strength, and courage, and confidence by each experience in which we really stop to look fear in the face ... we must do that which we think we cannot."*

Eleanor Roosevelt

Fear is paralysing, it is the enemy of progress. Fear can glue you on the spot. Through the belief work we did in Step 12, you may have started to reduce the impact of some of your fears. Well done. However, there may be some more ingrained beliefs and fears that you have yet to uncover. In this step, we will approach challenges from another angle and start asking "What are you scared of?". Don't worry if beliefs and fears start getting mixed up; the purpose of the work we are doing is to discover limitations and challenges. It doesn't really matter what you call them; what matters is that you become aware of them and how they are stopping you from being all that you can be.

# To get rid of fears, you often have to confront them

Dealing with fear often involves doing the things you are scared of doing. This is one of the bulletproof ways to see that the fear is unfounded and to lessen the hold it has on you. Just like challenging beliefs, you end up challenging the fear. Obviously, I'm not talking about the risk-taking type of fears that jeopardise your safety. I'm talking about the type of fears that hold you back in life. Let's say you get an opportunity to speak in public to advertise your new service but you are really scared of being up on stage. You have two options: you turn down the offer, stay at home and don't advertise your service, or you accept the offer. If you turn down the offer, fear will have "paralysed" you; it will have stopped you from getting ahead. On the other hand, if you accept the offer, you will have to work through your fear. It is unlikely that your fear will go away completely, but if you prepare, work through some visualisation exercises to gain some confidence, challenge your beliefs about what people will think of you, get excited about the opportunity and go ahead and present regardless, you will have made some progress and chances are that next time around you will be less frightened when a speaking opportunity arises.

I had a terrible fear of public speaking in my 20s. It came from being made to stand in front of the class in primary school to recite poetry. The main issue was that we didn't really get any form of training, we were just told to learn a poem and recite it in front of the class. This often meant a boring performance and a yawning audience. I grew up to intensely dislike all forms of public speaking. In my 30s this became a serious limitation at work so I sought help, but the thing that really sorted this out once and for all was when I got a job as a university lecturer. My first lecture was two hours long. I was so nervous and spoke so quickly that I ran out of material after an hour. So I called a break, went out of the room, hyperventilated a bit and asked myself "What would my best teacher now do?". I then decided to engage the class in a discussion on the stuff I'd just presented. This experience taught me that (a) it was possible to make mistakes and live, and (b) I could be resourceful. In fact, the discussion became animated and the students really enjoyed participating. I lectured for three years after that, made some more mistakes along the way (including saying the wrong thing and being corrected by a student in front of the class) and really enjoyed the experience. So, yes, jumping into the frying pan cured me of that fear once and for all – together with having lots of opportunities to practise, mess up and improve.

## It is normal to fear "new things"

Learn to appreciate that everyone when faced with a new situation is very likely to feel uncomfortable and even fearful. The vision of what you want for yourself represents a change in your life, so it will include new things, whether these are new behaviours, new situations, new people or new ways of working. Appreciate this before you start. Accept the fact that you will need to push through some discomfort to get there. No point hiding from this. Create a belief that you have what it takes to get ahead, that the people who succeed at getting what they want in life are not "special" – they just have more guts and staying power. Convince yourself that your only option when faced by fear is to push ahead. Believe that after a while you will start feeling more comfortable as you get used to the new activity. And be ready to screw up at times! My students probably liked me more because I did; it made me human.

## Sabotage

My love life was not great until my mid-30s. I didn't realise at the time, but I had a tendency to sabotage my chances of making a relationship work. I think this came from a couple of beliefs. I feared that a serious relationship would clip my wings and I wouldn't be able to do what I wanted in life. The other issue was that I had actually never seen a working relationship as my parents didn't get on and eventually divorced. So, I had no real example of what to do. This led to a belief that "making relationships work was impossible". So, rather than deal with the beliefs, the fears and the fact that I'd have to work at it, I just sabotaged every relationship I had until I ended up getting divorced when my daughter was only 18 months old. This was a very sad time but also a turning point. It took quite a lot of heartache to realise what was going on and to start doing something different.

Sabotage is an unconscious mechanism until you figure out what is going on. Being paralysed by fears means that you just get stuck; sabotage is worse because you actually move backwards by destroying things. Another example of this is the fear of success. Many people are frightened of succeeding without realising it. It's rarely success in itself they fear but rather the impact it will have on their lives. For example, they may think that success will have a negative impact on their friendships or their ability to spend time with their family.

To test if you fear success, think about what you want. Now think what life will be like when you have it. What will have changed? Is that type of change something you are afraid of? For example, let's say you want to be a successful actor. When you think about your goal and see yourself as a successful actor, you realise that your success may overshadow your partner who has been trying to succeed for years as a musician but has failed. In order not to upset your partner, you unconsciously sabotage your efforts so that you don't make it. Both of you can then "connect" through your lack of success. Sounds mad? It is. But ... it happens. A lot.

# Needs and values

Your fears and subsequent sabotage will be linked to your beliefs but also to your needs and values. As I said before, these things are closely intertwined and the point isn't to categorise them exactly. The point is to understand the challenges you face and do something about them.

We looked at values in Step 2. If this seems like a long time ago, please pull out your values exercise and refresh your memory. As discussed previously, if you value the time you spend with your family but you believe that getting what you want will take you away from them, you may well sabotage your chances. This doesn't necessarily mean that you have to abandon your goals because they might not align with your "family time", but it may mean rethinking your vision a little. If what you want involves travel, maybe you could take your family with you?

In addition to values, we all have needs that we consciously or unconsciously try to meet. They start with basic needs such as water, food and shelter and extend all the way to more complex needs around fulfilment.

# Satisfying your needs

A need is something that will make it difficult for you to function unless it is fulfilled, for example the need to be loved or respected or the need for peace. Therein lies the problem. An unconscious and unfulfilled need could be driving your actions and adversely impacting your ability to make things happen. Let me explain. I grew up in a family where there were beliefs that money was a limited resource that would eventually run out if we were not careful. This means that I'm very good at balancing a budget and I don't spend more than I earn. However, it does mean that I can be too cautious when it comes to money, and that I have a need for safety. In fact, I have a need to feel secure generally (remember that my parents didn't get on), not just when it comes to money. The trouble with this is that needing to feel secure doesn't always fit well with the fact that I'm self-employed and don't get a salaried income. I have to constantly work on this need and its impact, which may translate into putting a lot of effort into ensuring a constant stream of work rather than resting on my laurels. Probably not a bad thing for a freelancer anyway!

# Make it fly

Hopefully by now, you should be starting to become aware of your values, needs, beliefs, fears and sabotage and of their impact on your life and your ability to get what you want.

In the exercise below, we will look at identifying your needs.

> ## STEP 13 EXERCISE (PART 1)
> ## UNCOVER YOUR NEEDS
>
> 1. Look at the list below and select 10 needs. If it's a need for you, you should get an emotion when you

read the word (embarrassment, need to move on to the next word quickly, yearning, etc.).

2. Compare each need in your list of 10 to each other in the same way as you did with values, and narrow your list down to four. These will be the strongest needs for you. (There is a template on the website.)

## List of needs

| | |
|---|---|
| Be accepted (approved, popular, respected) | Be needed (improve others, be useful, be important) |
| To accomplish (achieve, realise, reach) | Duty (do the right thing, have a task, have a cause) |
| Be acknowledged (worthy, praised, appreciated) | Be free (unrestricted, autonomous, independent) |
| Be loved (cherished, preferred, adored) | Honesty (loyalty, no lying, no secrets) |
| Be right (correct, confirmed, advocated) | Order (perfection, symmetry, consistency) |
| Be cared for (get attention, be cared about, get gifts) | Peace (quietness, balance, agreement) |
| Certainty (clarity, promises, assurance) | Power (authority, strength, influence) |
| Be comfortable (luxury, abundance, prosperity) | Recognition (be noticed, get credit, be known for) |
| To communicate (be heard, informed, make a point) | Safety (security, protection, stability) |
| To control (command, be obeyed, correct others) | Work (performance, responsibility, make it happen) |

Now that you are aware of your needs, let's move to figuring out what fears your vision brings to the surface and how these relate to your needs and values.

## STEP 13 EXERCISE (PART 2)
## DEALING WITH FEAR AND SABOTAGE

1. Review the entries in your challenges log. Now think of what you are afraid of, and if the issue is linked to an existing entry, just expand the "description" and the "impact" to clearly include the fear but also make a new entry in the "what will I do about this?" box, so that we can investigate and address the fear separately if need be. Otherwise, if you have uncovered a new fear, then make a new entry.

2. You should now have some fears listed in your challenges log. For each fear, think through what the belief behind it is and list it in the description box. You can also add the needs or values at play if that makes sense.

3. If you are confused by the exercise at any point, just take a look at the worked examples on the website.

# DO IT!

1. Get hold of your plan and review the tasks you have progressed according to what you set out to do in the previous step. If you have completed some tasks, change their status to complete. If some have slipped, adjust your plan. If you have slipped, ask yourself whether you may be sabotaging your efforts.

2. Decide what tasks you will complete next and build some time in your week to complete those tasks. If you have come up with some actions you'll take to deal with challenges, add them to your plan.

3. Build some time each morning and/or evening to sit in silence and visualise what you want (see the exercise in Step 3).

4. Build some time to look after YOU in your schedule.

# Step 14

## Increase your self-confidence

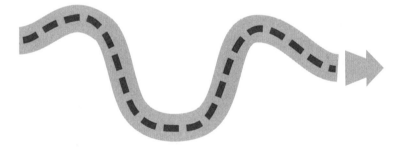

*"Self-confidence is the first requisite to great undertakings."*

Samuel Johnson

In this step, I'd like to look at things from a different perspective. Rather than focus on dealing with challenges, I'd like to work with you to raise your self-confidence, so that when obstacles come your way you will be dealing with them from a position of strength. This position of strength will come from believing in yourself, feeling good and grounded and knowing that you are able to handle difficulties.

# Personal development happens holistically

The great thing about personal development is that it doesn't happen in a linear organised fashion, so although we are using the steps to work on ourselves, there are many different ways to get to the same place. This is why the steps may sometimes appear to overlap and why, when you successfully change, you may find it hard to pinpoint exactly what action led to the shift. This is also why there are a variety of approaches to change. I find this extremely useful because it allows me to present a variety of tools and viewpoints, increasing the chance that some of them will resonate with you personally.

I said at the beginning of this book that you cannot change yourself by following a set of instructions. You cannot say "fear go away", then find that it has. Sometimes you will get "ah ha" moments and a big shift will occur, but more often than not a fear will go away as a result of your becoming aware of it, confronting it, shifting a belief or addressing a need *all at once*. Ultimately, it doesn't really matter what technique or exercise worked. What is important is the outcome, the fact that you now believe in yourself and your vision and through this you are creating the momentum necessary to move towards what you really want.

# Increase your self-confidence

You can increase your self-confidence using many of the techniques we have already covered, and here's an opportunity to bring them all together in a neatly organised fashion (you can't organise their impact but you can organise the techniques!).

# Look after YOU

Look after your body, your health and your mind. Mix with people who energise you with their happiness and positivity. Feed your mind information that supports it in staying balanced and positive. Protect your resources and build a reserve. Get rid of stuff you don't need, delegate tasks and create some space in your life. Find time to connect with nature and other people. Find some time to sit in silence and focus on your breath. Sleep.

# Act

Don't just think about stuff; *do* something. If you are looking for the perfect partner, do your affirmations but also go where they are likely to hang out. They won't find you in your living room. Put all the chances on your side. If you're afraid, do something about it. Try stuff out – maybe a little bit at a time, or jump right in. Pretend you are not scared of that thing, visualise yourself confidently doing what you're afraid of doing, then do it. Tell people you are about to do something and ask them for help. Get someone to hold your hand as you try something that scares you.

# Focus on what is working and on the present

If you want to feel healthier, focus on how the changes you are making are starting to work. Focus on the fact that you just completed a 30-minute run rather than agonise over the bar of chocolate you just ate. If you feel nothing is working, go back over sections of this book you've found inspiring and start again. Remember that each new day is an opportunity to do something different. I know this is hard, but try to let go of the past and focus on what you can do now, what actions you could take today.

Take one day at a time and focus on what is working on that day. Look for evidence that things are working in areas other than your project and be grateful. Try to catch your thoughts and to stop negative cycles of thoughts about yourself and your plans. If you find yourself sabotaging your chances, stop, notice what you are doing, then start again.

It can be hard to pick yourself up and start again. Unfortunately, there are no alternatives. If something doesn't work, all you can do is find a way of making it work. If you make a mistake, the only thing you can do is let it go and do better next time. If you liked the section on meditation, think back to the concept of "living in the moment" because ultimately this is all you can change. The past is gone and the future is not here yet.

# Remind yourself of your success

Keep a gratitude journal where you list everything you are grateful for in your life. Recognise that you brought all this to yourself and you can bring some more. Pull out your plan and look at all the tasks and actions you've successfully completed. If something isn't quite working, sit still, focus on your breath and ask for guidance. If something is not working, keep trying different things until it works. Tell people about your successes and enlist them to remind you of them when you feel like giving up.

# Keep challenging your beliefs and living "as if"

Keep uncovering what is stopping you. Keep trying new techniques for understanding yourself better. When you find limiting beliefs, look for evidence that challenges them. Pretend that you don't have the belief and act "as if". Pretend you are an actor and your job is to act "as if" that belief wasn't there. Then watch what happens.

# Get your needs met

Figure out what your needs are and get them met outside your vision so that you can work on your project need-free. Brainstorm ways to satisfy your needs that can be combined with looking after YOU. For example, if you want recognition, take up a competitive sport. Build a reserve and satisfy your need for security. Do some charity work and meet your need to be needed.

# Visualise yourself succeeding

I can't say this more: every day visualise yourself achieving what you want, feel how you will feel, see what you will see, taste or touch if appropriate. And make sure you put yourself *in* the vision, not on the outside. Look through your own eyes. Feel the energy that the vision creates and use it to propel yourself forward.

# Do your affirmations

Write your affirmations down on cards and pin them in places where you will see them - on your computer, on the bathroom mirror, in the shower, on the fridge. Pin them where you *need* to see them, for example health ones in the kitchen. Use them to encourage yourself to do what you set out to do. "I always eat healthy food" pinned on the kitchen wall may be all it takes to motivate you. I have a set of work goals pinned down behind my computer and some good affirmations about happiness and opportunities on my bathroom mirror.

# Make it fly

As I wrote the previous paragraphs, an interesting thing happened. I felt more and more positive about life, and energy started moving around my body. I really hope that reading the words has had the same effect on you!

Let's now give you an opportunity to develop ways to satisfy your needs and weaken or shift your limiting beliefs, and as a result to increase your confidence in your ability to make the things you want happen in your life.

> **STEP 14**
>
> **INCREASING YOUR SELF-CONFIDENCE**
>
> 1. Look at the list of ways you can use to increase your confidence and identify the area that requires the most work and that you are currently neglecting. Focus on that area for the next month.

Make a note on your plan that this is what you are going to do, so that the commitment is visible. At the end of the month or any other set period that works for you, focus on another area. What I'm trying to do is to get you to form good habits through repetition.

2. To remind yourself, wear a bracelet or keep a pebble in your pocket. Use your bracelet or pebble to remind you of what you are working on. For example, I wear a bracelet to remind myself to have positive thoughts throughout the day. I still have negative thoughts, but looking at my bracelet encourages me to stop and try to think differently. And yes, sometimes I get used to the bracelet and have to change the prop!

3. Whether you become more confident working on tasks on your plan or you use the above method to adopt a new habit, it doesn't matter. You can do this any way you like. As we said, it's the outcome we are after. We want you to feel more grounded and more confident. How you get there is up to you.

## DO IT!

1. Get hold of your plan and review the tasks you have progressed according to what you set out to do in the previous step. If you have completed some tasks, change their status to complete. If some have slipped, adjust your plan. Always question why you are slipping. Don't beat yourself up but do look at whether you are sabotaging your efforts.

2. Decide what tasks you will complete next and build some time in your week to complete those tasks. If you haven't added issues and risks tasks to your plan, review your challenges log and plan some tasks around addressing issues and mitigating risks.

3. Commit to building a confidence-enhancing habit over the next month or whatever set period works for you.

4. Build some time each morning and/or evening to sit in silence and visualise what you want (see the exercise in Step 3).

5. Build some time to look after YOU in your schedule.

# Step 15
## Take responsibility

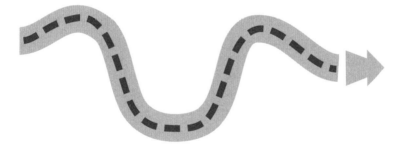

*"The price of greatness is responsibility."*
Winston Churchill

I showed you some examples of how the world around you is impacted by your thoughts and actions, and how therefore you are responsible for creating many of your experiences. If you accept this, then you will also accept that taking responsibility for your thoughts and your actions is key to getting what you want.

*But ... hang on a minute, what about accidents, what's happening in the world and other people? Surely these also impact my reality.* Yes, these do impact your life as well. However, even then you still hold a large chunk of the power. Although you cannot directly change other people and the events in the world, you can choose how you react to them. And the way you act, as we've seen, influences the behaviours of the people around you. So, indirectly, you can influence other people. In addition, if something external affects your vision, you can choose to do something different and take a different path. This, of course, is not always easy, though a choice does exist. You can choose to be a victim or you can pick yourself up and try something different. It is up to you.

# Take responsibility for your thoughts

Whether you believe that you create your reality or not, you have to admit that if you spend every waking hour telling yourself that you won't get what you want and you won't succeed, you are unlikely to be in the correct state of mind to make your vision come true. From this day onward, I would like you to commit to taking responsibility for your thoughts and your actions by keeping a watching brief over what is going on in your head, what you are telling people and how you are behaving. Do you think people will believe in your vision if you can't talk about it confidently? Unlikely.

*"If you think you can do a thing or think you can't do a thing, you're right."*

*Henry Ford*

Remember the getting promoted example. It started with a belief about "not being good enough". The belief then got translated into thoughts. These thoughts caused the person to drop some little hints of what was going on in their head in everyday conversation. Those little hints were picked up by people at work, leading them to form a view. That view was in line with the belief: "person is not ready for promotion" or "doesn't really want promotion".

Part of the "Do it!" section in each step encourages you to visualise what you want twice a day for 10 minutes; we've also discussed the use of affirmations in some of the previous steps. If you have not started visualising and affirming, now is the time to commit. Go on, give it a try. Visualisation and affirmation are good ways to influence your thoughts.

# Yes, but ...

Ah, excuses. "I would but …". Every time you use the word "but" in a sentence, pay attention to what comes after. This person that jeopardises your plans may well live inside you. Do you really have to wait for your kids to be grown up, for your boss to be nicer, for your partner to be more supportive? Or is this just a way not to take responsibility and face the fear of having to make a different choice? Your boss may never be nicer. Will you really wait for something that may never happen to get what you want in life? Will you really give your power away to someone who isn't nice to you? However much you may not want the trouble, you could find another job and another boss, or you could become self-employed, or you could just act differently around your boss and see if their behaviour changes. Watch out that you don't base your ability to do something on other people changing their behaviours: this is a sure sign of not taking ownership of a situation.

# Complaining habits

Do you complain? Complaining is a sign of not taking responsibility for something. If you catch yourself complaining, dig a little and if you find a fear or limiting belief at play, go back to the relevant steps and do a little bit more work. If you find no fear or limiting belief, it may just be that your confidence has dipped. Maybe things have not been going your way for a while or maybe you're just not feeling your best. No serious fear or belief at play, just a series of unfortunate events and we end up in a negative cycle. "Well, I tried 10 times and it didn't work." OK, that's disheartening, but let's analyse "how" you tried. Could you try a different way? What if number

11 is the one that works? Was it really 10 times? Often when people say "I tried lots of things", it only means three separate things. Notice the areas where you say "yes but" or where you complain. Are you giving your power away?

Accept that it will not be plain sailing every day. Some days will be challenging. Try to learn the lesson and encourage yourself to move on. You tried a new way to sell your new product and it didn't work. Instead of thinking that you are a failure at selling, think that you have just learnt one way that doesn't work very well. Think back to the difference between optimists and pessimists and where they allocate failure. If you are struggling with sales generally and a few of your attempts have failed, try going on a course or asking people for feedback. Why did they not want to buy? You may find an opportunity to improve your product or an opportunity to improve your sales techniques.

# Other people and the world at large

You can take responsibility and choose how you react to other people and to the external world by building some boundaries around yourself and your project. You do this by becoming very clear about what is acceptable to you and what isn't. This is important because once you know where you will compromise and where you won't, it becomes a lot simpler to say "no". The clearer you are about what is important and what you are not willing to compromise, the easier it will be to take responsibility and to say "no" when you are asked to do something that you don't really want to do. If you've made yourself a promise that nothing will jeopardise your weekly sessions at the gym, it will be easier to say "no" when you get a request to do something else at the same time.

# Make it fly

Now let's look at some areas where you could take more responsibility in your life. Take your exercise materials out and follow the instructions below.

## STEP 15

## OPPORTUNITIES TO TAKE RESPONSIBILITY

1. Think about areas of your life where you could take more responsibility. Here are some generic questions to help your thinking.

   - Do you say "yes" to people when you mean "no" and then get resentful? For example, do you agree to go somewhere with your best friend because you don't want to disappoint them when you'd rather be doing something else, then get angry later?

   - What do you complain about? Is there an area of your life you constantly complain about? Is it possible that you are doing this to get attention? Is it possible that you are doing this because you are scared to do something about the problem?

   - Do you have bad habits that drain your energy? Do you eat badly? Smoke? Drink more than you should? Go to bed really late? We will talk about distractions and the things you tolerate in the next step, but it may be helpful to start thinking why you do this.

   - Do you use excuses rather than face up to a fear? Every "yes but ..." is worth investigating. Do you promise to take some action but when reviewing your plan find that the task is simply not getting done?

   - Do your thoughts and actions support your project? Pay attention to what you think about, how you talk about your dream.

2. Pull out your challenges log and make an entry for each area where you give your power away and how you think this may impact your goals. Find ways to take your power back.

# DO IT!

1. Get hold of your plan and review the tasks you have progressed according to what you set out to do in the previous step. If you have completed some tasks, change their status to complete. If some have slipped, adjust your plan. If you are seriously slipping, ask yourself where you need to take more responsibility.

2. Decide what tasks you will complete next and build some time in your week to complete those tasks. If you haven't added issues and risks tasks to your plan, review your challenges log and plan some tasks around addressing issues and mitigating risks.

3. Build some time each morning and/or evening to sit in silence and visualise what you want (see the exercise in Step 3).

4. Build some time to look after YOU in your schedule.

# Step 16

# Minimise distractions

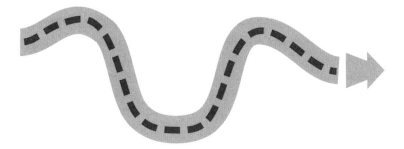

"In the absence of clearly-defined goals, we become strangely loyal to performing daily trivia until ultimately we become enslaved by it."

Robert Heinlein

We have covered several types of barriers to success: fears, beliefs, lack of motivation, lack of confidence, giving your power away, etc. The last challenge I'd like to cover is that of distractions. You know the one. You sit at your desk with the intention of working on your new website. Three hours later, you have made zero progress; however, all your emails have been answered, your Facebook status has been updated six times and you've had a 20-minute chat with your best friend. These are called distractions, and with life becoming more and more hectic there are likely to be lots calling on your valuable time. If it isn't email and Facebook, it may be the pile of washing, the grass that needs mowing, the friend you haven't called for weeks, etc. Just fill in the gaps with your own preferred distractions.

# Is housework really more important than your vision?

I'm not suggesting that you give up on all the jobs you need to do around the house, as this is unlikely to make you popular at home and to encourage your family and friends to support you when you work on achieving your goals (and you need that!). What I am saying is that if you have set aside time to move your plan forward, then at that time you need to be working on your project. If knowing that the washing needs doing is going to stop you focusing, then do the washing and come back to your project afterwards. Manage your time. However, it's good to remind yourself that there will always be something that needs doing. There may be a need to learn to tolerate housework not getting done immediately. Let's face it, it's hardly going to go away. You *can* do it later.

Or do what I do and use housework as thinking time. Put the washing in the machine and when the time comes to take the clothes out, use that time to take a small break to reflect on an issue. The same applies to mowing the lawn. All those activities make great thinking time. I often get inspiration when cooking or see the solution to a problem when my mind is focused elsewhere. But be careful: if you have too many of these activities calling on your time, consider hiring a housekeeper or a gardener. I read somewhere years ago that every hour I spent cleaning the house gave me nothing whilst every hour I spent working on my goals took me closer to them. As I could afford it, why was I choosing to clean? I've had someone clean my house ever since and whatever guilt I had about hiring someone is long gone.

# You can turn the phone off, yes, you can

Here's a revolutionary idea: if email or the phone is what distracts you, *turn them off*. You absolutely do not have to be available every minute of the day. I'm old enough to remember a time when we didn't have mobile phones. Guess what? If people really needed to find me, they did. If you are worried about emergencies, then maybe leave the phone on but get an answering machine. That way you can screen the calls and you won't end up getting caught into a long conversation with someone just because you haven't got the courage to tell them you'll call them back. Just don't pick up, and when you're done working on your project then call them back. I bet you, they'll still be ready for a chat and you can enthusiastically share your progress with them rather than spend an hour complaining about the lack of it.

# Value the time spent on your vision

Book time to work on your goals in your agenda and do not let anything take that time away from you. The time you spend on your project is invaluable; it is what will move you forward, and when you move forward you gain momentum, and when you have momentum you'll often start feeling that things are moving ahead by themselves. Rather than worry about the distractions, try to remove them as much as you can. Take the thing that distracts you away, pay someone to deal with it, forget about it for a set period of time or address the issue. Try to make it impossible to get distracted; turn the Internet or the phone off. Make a very strong commitment to yourself that when you work on your goals, this is all that you do.

If you need to, also make this clear to the people around you. Set some clear expectations. Your time is precious and right now you are working on your goals. You will pay the others lots of attention later, but this will be after you have spent a productive hour moving your plans forward. Maybe explain to them that if you don't progress towards what you want, you will feel down and you will not be very good company anyway. However, once you've made some progress, you'll feel proud and you'll be able to spend some good time with them.

# When distractions hide more serious problems

If you are not managing to ward off distractions with these suggestions then you may have a more serious issue. If you find that you simply cannot focus, it may be time to start asking yourself some serious questions. What are you afraid of? What are the consequences of your vision becoming real? Chances are you will be able to tie this back to one of your fears or limiting beliefs, and if you haven't done anything to weaken them, now is the time.

# Make it fly

Time for a quick exercise.

**STEP 16 EXERCISE**

**IDENTIFY DISTRACTIONS**

1. By now, you should be working on your project regularly and have booked regular time slots in your diary. More importantly, working on getting what you want should now be part of your everyday life. If you haven't established a regular schedule, it is time to do it. As I said previously, there's nothing like writing things down: physically make appointments in your diary for time when you'll work on making what you want happen.

2. Take out your challenges log and enter all the things that distract you from working on your project, then how you will "remove" them.

# DO IT!

1. Get hold of your plan and review the tasks you have progressed according to what you set out to do in the previous step. If you have completed some tasks, change their status to complete. If some have slipped, ask yourself why, then adjust your plan. If you keep slipping the same task, it's time to wonder what is really stopping you from progressing this task and to make a real commitment to move it forward in the next few days.

2. Decide what tasks you will complete next and build some time in your week to complete those tasks. If you haven't added issues and risks tasks to your plan, review your challenges log and plan some tasks around addressing issues and mitigating risks.

3. Make sure time to spend on your vision is booked in your diary.

4. Build some time each morning and/or evening to sit in silence and visualise what you want (see the exercise in Step 3).

5. Make time to look after YOU.

# Step 17

# Take stock, really go for it

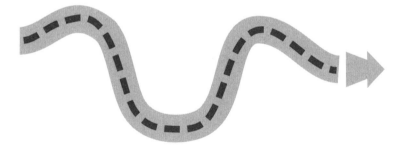

*"Go for it. The future is promised to no one."*
Wayne Dyer

We are now more than half-way through the book. This step is therefore a great place to stop and think, and before we move further ahead let's spend some time taking stock. Let's review together the great progress you've been making. If you have followed the steps and done all the exercises, you will now have the following:

- A very clear picture of where you are headed which you can use to (a) check that each action is actually taking you forward to that picture rather than further from it, and (b) visualise to keep your motivation and confidence high.

- An approach and a plan with a clear set of tasks, a good idea of the resources you'll require to put the plan in place and an estimate of how long it will take you to complete the work. You will have also started working on some of the tasks through the "Do it!" section included from Step 8 onwards.

- An understanding of the people who are likely to have an interest in your project and how you can engage them and get their support.

- A challenges log identifying the things that are likely to trip you up as well as ways to deal with them. You will have also started to address those challenges through the "Do it!" sections. More importantly, you will have started becoming more and more aware of your behaviours and how they hinder or support you.

- An opportunity log listing things that you can pull on to increase your motivation and confidence or use to speed up getting what you want.

- You may also have a diary with appointments for moving your plans forward, a gratitude journal, lots of affirmation cards dotted around your house, an established "visualisation practice", a new diet and an exercise regime. Who knows, you may also have completely de-cluttered your garage!

## This feels great!

At this point in the book, you are likely to have been working two angles in parallel: you will have been developing and refining your plan and challenges log, whilst at the same time taking action based on both of these. You may have not yet progressed the most involved tasks on your plan;

however, by the very act of working through the exercises, you will have started to make things happen. Congratulate yourself.

# Clarity and action

We discussed at the beginning of the book that it was important to be clear before taking action fully, otherwise there was a risk that we would squander our valuable resources. At this point in the book, I would hope that what you want and the plans to get there are fairly clear and that the areas where you wish to take action are fully defined. This is particularly important if there is money involved. From Part 4, I will encourage you to really go for it. So, to ensure that you are ready, I would like you to conduct a quick review. Pull out your exercise book or computer and let's see just how far you've come.

---

## STEP 17

## REVIEW

1. Get hold of all the materials you've produced to date. If they're in electronic form, print them out.

2. If you have more than one version of your plan, your challenge and opportunity logs, print only the latest version.

3. Read everything and make a note of what comes to mind as you read or adjust your material accordingly.

4. Ask yourself if there is something missing from your plan, your challenges log or your opportunity log. Is the way to deal with each challenge included in your plan? Are the activities to look after YOU on your plan or in your diary?

5. Spend some proper time reviewing everything and ensuring that it is as accurate and complete as possible.

6. Get excited – you're doing really well!

---

# The map to get what you want – your plan

Your plan is what you use to guide all the actions that you take. It should therefore include activities to move your vision forward but also activities to address all the challenges you have identified to date. For example, if you have listed "get myself a coach" as a way to work through limiting beliefs, you need to make sure that your plan includes the activities needed to find a coach, interview them, hire them and attend coaching sessions. The same is true if you want to buy an answering machine to screen calls when you are working on your project: make sure you add to your plan that you will find and buy one.

You may now be thinking that you don't need to record everything on your plan. Of course you don't, but my advice to you is that you do. I believe that the fact that you write down an activity and track its progress actually helps formalise that activity in your mind. It makes it real. I don't think that just telling yourself that you will remember to do something is as powerful. You may remember to do it and then you will have saved the two minutes it would have taken to add it to your plan. However, I'm not sure that gaining two minutes is actually worth the risk of forgetting to do what you meant to do, so just record everything on your plan.

I interviewed my friend Nadia for this book. Her big project is to set up a website where creative people can share and promote their talent. One key challenge she identified was the fact that she "had lots of stuff in her head and getting it down on paper would really help". She does have a plan but it's not recorded anywhere, so sometimes she finds it hard to make sure she works equally on the things she likes (marketing) and the things she doesn't like (legal). If you're interested in Nadia's work and have a particular talent you'd like to share, you can find her at www.talentreel.co.uk.

# Ticking things off builds momentum

Another reason for planning every task is that ticking them off by setting their status to "complete" feels great. You can, of course, tick off tasks in your mind, but it won't have the same effect. Let's use this example to draw a parallel: to get what you want, you have to take it from an idea and push it to the real world. Isn't it interesting that there is more chance you'll take action if you have committed the action to paper in the real world rather than kept it as a thought in your mind? You can spend some time reflecting on this.

# Where to now?

You should now have a very good understanding of what you want and the challenges you will face but also the reasons why you want this and what you will need to do to keep moving ahead. The next part is about really going for it, using everything you've learnt. If you need to go back on some of the steps or do some more work before you move ahead, feel free to do so.

Now go for it!

## DO IT!

1. Get hold of your plan and review the tasks you have progressed according to what you set out to do in the previous step. If you have completed some tasks, change their status to complete. If some have slipped, ask yourself what you will do to get them done and adjust your plan.

2. Decide what tasks you will complete next (the ones that have slipped?) and build some time in your week to complete those tasks. If you haven't added issues and risks tasks to your plan, review your risks and issues log and plan some tasks around addressing issues and mitigating risks. Really go for it – maybe pick a difficult task you've been avoiding.

3. Build some time each morning and/or evening to sit in silence and visualise what you want (see the exercise in Step 3).

4. Build some time to look after YOU in your schedule.

# PART 4

# Get going and stay going

"Ideas are easy. It's the execution of ideas that really separates the sheep from the goats."

Sue Grafton

At this stage in the book, I hope that I will have instilled in you a habit to "make it fly" through writing things down, planning tasks in your diary or plan, and committing to move your vision forward or to remove an obstacle. This is where the phrase "The only thing standing between you and your dream is YOU" becomes important. If you have yet to take action, I would encourage you to go back to the beginning now and to commit to working through the exercises. There is no point in moving full steam ahead if none of the previous building blocks are in place. Sorry.

If, on the other hand, you have completed the exercises, followed the instructions, started taking action and feel excited to crank things up a notch, let's go!

# Step 18

## When small steps lead to big jumps

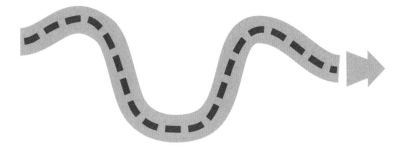

*"Faith is taking the first step even when you don't see the whole staircase."*

Martin Luther King Jr

Every change I've ever made, whether in my life or in organisations, started with small steps that eventually built up to the vision. None involved a single massive "big bang" task, so for me, success comes from continually moving forward, from taking action every day. Yes, at times, when in flow, it will feel like I'm moving in leaps and bounds, but this is usually down to the outcomes of all my small actions converging and things starting to take shape at the same time rather than to some massive amount of effort invested in a single task. In this step, I want to encourage you to break things down and take small but regular actions.

# Small steps make visions seem more manageable

The idea that getting what you want is the result of a lot of small actions is good for the soul. It means you can build your vision one brick at a time, removing the need to find the one perfect large step that will take you there in one clean swoop. Looking at things this way will also help you do away with the fear of taking a single huge jump over the gap that stands between you and your goals. The giant leaps will come but they will come over time and as a result of all the small steps. You'll see them as massive leaps when you look back. I like Seth Godin's expression "drip, drip, drip, you win".

# But I want to be there now!

If you are impatient, find a way to enjoy the journey or turn your lack of patience into energy to move all the small tasks forward. Don't worry about not being there yet. Start enjoying what you're learning along the way. Start enjoying the journey. After all, if you have a fear of success, it would be good to get used to your new life at a pace that allows you to realise the impact of it on your present life and to make the appropriate adjustments. This, I think, is a question of how you look at things. Ask yourself what would happen if all of a sudden your dream life was yours and you had not spent any time thinking things through. An example of this is the lottery winner who gets a big win before they have learnt how to "be" rich in their mind and addressed their limiting beliefs around money. They are usually not rich for very long.

# Drip, drip makes the change stick

A good example of how small steps can lead to big and permanent results is successful weight loss programmes. A good weight loss programme will encourage daily action in several areas at the same time: food choices, portion sizes, exercise, mind work to remain positive. Weight will be lost in small increments every week until it builds up to a larger number. If you stick with the programme, you will lose weight but also acquire some good habits around what to eat, how much to eat, exercising and looking after yourself. The combination of daily action over months is what will lead to good and hopefully permanent results. Please note that I am talking about losing weight for someone without any significant psychological or physical issues.

In the case of weight loss, the small steps approach can be discouraging if results are not immediately visible. I still believe that it's the best way to go about it and I would encourage you to fill in your progress report (we'll discuss this at the end of the step) so that you can notice things changing and rejoice in the smallest of achievements. Trust me, small achievements over time will add up to big ones. Keep up the faith in yourself.

# Small steps guide your unconscious

When I look back, I am often amazed at how much progress small steps have led me to make and how close to my plan things have turned out. This is another area where having a written plan is essential (you can't refer back to something that is in your head). Once you start being clear about what you want and taking action in that direction, your unconscious, the world, the universe, God, call it what you want, starts to conspire to take you there. If you don't like the notion of a God guiding you, just call it your subconscious.

# Small steps create momentum

Small steps create momentum by encouraging you to take regular action. Take an example where you have two ways to get what you want. In option one, you need to take one very big step. In option two, you need to take a series of regular but smaller steps. You choose number one and complete your single task but unfortunately things don't work out. There's no progress and no momentum and your motivation is low. It takes you a month to recover and you have to start again from scratch. In another scenario, you choose the second option; three small steps are successful but one fails. Never mind: you're moving forward, you have momentum, so you create an alternative small step and rectify your course. Can you see how option two keeps momentum and motivation on the up?

Doing what I just did and saying that three small steps moved you forward is called measuring progress. Measuring progress, as in the above example, helps demonstrate that things are working. This is where the momentum and motivation come from. To be able to see that things are working, you need a record of where you started, clarity on where you are going and a plan listing the actions you'll take to plug the gap. Through the work you've done, you've got all the tools in hand. To create momentum and keep you motivated, we will start to formally note "progress" as part of our regular work.

# Break everything down

Not only can you break your action plan down into manageable chunks, you can also break down how you deal with challenges. Let's say you come across a big obstacle: the venue for the 50th birthday party you've spent six months planning burns down two weeks before the event. You can focus on the size of the problem and be frozen by fear, or you can start working on small actions that could possibly resolve the issue. Even with a couple of weeks to go, you can look around for another venue, enlist the help of friends and family to find somewhere else, hold the party in your house or someone else's house, change the date, hold it outside in the garden, etc. Hopefully, breaking the challenge down and kicking off different strands of action will make you more confident in hoping for a solution and as a result in finding one.

Breaking something into small pieces helps size an outcome or a problem so that it appears achievable and, as a result, you become excited, motivated and passionate. When the pieces are too large, we often feel overwhelmed by their size and complexity. When you break goals down, the task or challenge becomes more realistic. It is said that elephants must be eaten one bite at a time. I'm not sure I like the image that comes to mind on this one, but nevertheless, the statement is true.

# Make it fly

In this exercise, we will ensure that you feel comfortable with the size of the tasks on your plan.

---

**STEP 18 EXERCISE**

## SMALL STEPS AND REPORTS

1. Pull out your plan and your challenges log.

2. Make sure all tasks are broken down into achievable steps you feel comfortable with. See yourself performing the tasks: does this seem like something you can do?

3. Look at the actions on your plan that relate to your challenges log and do the same thing.

4. Get hold of the Progress Report template from the website and fill it in as explained in the "Do it!" section. Commit to measure your progress on a regular basis, maybe once a week.

---

## DO IT!

1. Get hold of your plan and review the tasks you have progressed according to what you set out to do in the last step. If you have completed some tasks, change their status to complete. If some have slipped, ask yourself why and adjust your plan.

2. Download the Progress Report template from the website and enter a name for your project and the date. Then enter the key milestones (the key achievements that will come out from performing the tasks on your plan), the activities you completed this week and the activities you plan to complete next week.

3. Build some time in your week to complete next week's tasks.

4. Enter the key challenges on your progress report and how you will look to address them.

5. Add some decisions you have to make this week and a comment to encourage you to move forward. To help, you could pretend that you are reporting to someone else on your progress, or you could start reporting to a friend or to your life partner.

6. Fill in the "How am I feeling?" box and the "Looking after me" area. Build some "looking after YOU" activities in your diary.

7. Build some time each morning and/or evening to sit in silence and visualise what you want (see the exercise in Step 3).

# Step 19

## Celebrate success, stay positive

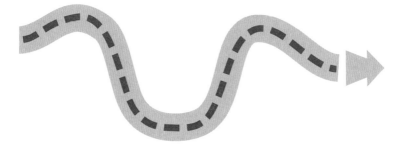

*"The more you praise and celebrate your life, the more there is in life to celebrate."*

Oprah Winfrey

We've talked quite a bit about difficulties; however, there will not only be issues, there will be achievements and successes – times when you will feel that you are moving ahead, and feedback from the world to prove that you are. It might be the day you sell your first piece of hand-made jewellery or find the perfect venue for your wedding.

Hopefully, by now, you have developed a regular habit of updating your plan and booking activities in your diary and you've made a good start on the progress report. I hope that as you move forward, you are taking some time to celebrate. If you are working well with your success partner, maybe they are giving you encouragement as well. Maybe the two of you meet up regularly to see how well you're doing. If you aren't taking time to notice your progress, it is important that you start as soon as you can. Recognising that your efforts are worth it will help you stay motivated. In this step, I will encourage you to appreciate your achievements and celebrate your success.

# Enjoy the journey

Do not wait to reach your ultimate goal to feel happy; enjoy the journey there. Try to make your experience a positive one. Remember how our attitude affects our relationships. What do you think happens to people who "miserably" build their dreams? That's right, they attract misery rather than joy and happiness. Just think about how much you want to hang around miserable people and how much help and support you want to give them. If you happily work on building your vision, not only will you enjoy the journey, you will also attract support, help and opportunities. Celebrating your achievements will help you stay focused on the positive.

# Celebrate responsibly

A small word of warning: when I say "celebrate", I do not mean go crazy each time you achieve a small step on the plan. Make your celebration match your achievements. Wait for the big celebration but have small celebrations along the way. If you've just successfully written the scope of what you want and you feel good about it, go and have a nice coffee with a friend and share your success with them. If you've just opened the doors to your new shop and the customers are flooding in, go out for dinner with your partner. This seems common sense, but it is easy as the going gets tough to want to make ourselves feel good for even the tiniest of achievements. The trouble is that if you celebrate too much, you may end up doing that rather than moving your plan forward.

# Why should I celebrate success?

- Celebrating success is a physical demonstration that you are achieving your goals. It's a way of acknowledging that what you are doing is working.

- Celebrating your success is a reward for having had to work hard through some challenges. It's the confirmation that it was well worth the effort.

- When you stop to celebrate, you become re-energised and get an opportunity to reflect on what you've learnt along the way and possibly to refocus your efforts. Celebrating your achievements is a positive way to take stock.

- Through noticing your success, you will become motivated to continue forward. If things are working, you'll be encouraged to do more. Who knows, your success may also give you the courage that has eluded you up to now to break through a significant limit or fear.

- When you stop to celebrate your success, you are sending the world and your success partners the message that you are well on the way to getting what you want, that you are serious about it.

- Acknowledging your success and achievements keeps you focused on the positive.

- Seeing that things are working does wonders for momentum and flow.

# Make it fly

Let's now look at creating a positive environment from your achievements and successes.

## STEP 19 EXERCISE
## CELEBRATE SUCCESS

1. Pull out your latest progress report, identify your latest achievement and add a rewarding activity to next week's plan.

2. If you haven't got into the habit of keeping a gratitude journal, start one now, and every night before you go to sleep, write down five things you are grateful for.

3. List your achievements on one page in your gratitude journal and re-read them regularly. Or you could print out a copy of your plan and highlight the tasks that are complete – whatever works to mark your progress.

# DO IT!

1. Get hold of your plan and commit to moving some of the new tasks forward in the next week. Enter in your progress report for this week.

2. Build some time in your week to complete next week's tasks.

3. Extract the key issues and risks and how you will look to address them. Update your progress report.

4. Add some decisions you have to make this week to your progress report and a comment to encourage you to move forward.

5. Build some time each morning and/or evening to sit in silence and visualise what you want (see the exercise in Step 3). Add this to your daily work.

6. Every night, think of five things from your day you are grateful for and write them down in your gratitude journal.

7. Book time in your diary to look after YOU – maybe a nice nature walk next Sunday?

# Step 20

## Motivation, persistence and daily work

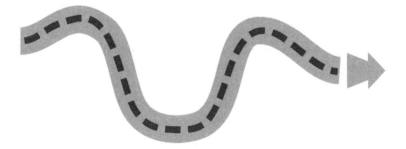

*"The person who makes a success of living is the one who sees his goal steadily and aims for it unswervingly. That is dedication."*
Cecil B. De Mille

The trick is to continually move towards your vision in everything you say and do. We've been using our plan and diary to take action. In this step, we will do a bit more work to make sure your project is part of your daily life so that you take action every day, but before we do so, let's have a look at motivation and persistence.

# Motivation and persistence

To help you get to your vision, I have to make sure that what I tell you and the exercises I set make you want to move forward and take action and do it persistently in spite of the obstacles you meet along the way. Although I cast the net a bit wider in the method, for example you also have to aim your action in the right direction, the key principle is still that I have to get you moving and keep you there.

Motivation and persistence work together. If you are motivated, you will want to persist and often you will increase your motivation by persisting. For example, when you first start on the road to getting what you want, things are likely to be looking up (you haven't faced an obstacle yet); your motivation will be high and it will be easy to persist in taking action. Then bang, an obstacle comes along. Your motivation dips. You sit down and do your visualisation exercises to remind you just how much you want this thing. Your energy starts flowing again and you get an idea on how to tackle the obstacle. You successfully remove the obstacle and your motivation goes up again. If this doesn't work the first time, you find a different way to remain motivated and to persist with the obstacle. Maybe this time you also enlist the help of one of your success partners. It's a virtuous cycle: action impacts your motivation which in turn encourages you to persist with your goal.

# Do you keep at it?

Persistence is a skill you will need to develop if you are to see your vision come to life. Persistence is the thing that will keep you going if you fail at first or when you are frightened by the risks. It is the essential ingredient to success and achievement. What I would like you to do now is examine your life and identify times when you have persisted and succeeded in making a change, so that you can get a feel for what this means for you. You should also get some proof that you can be persistent.

Let's take the example of someone who wants to stop smoking. They first decide they wish to stop and think of a bunch of motivational factors: they will be healthier, have more money, have white teeth, have great-smelling breath, etc. They take the first step and on day one they manage not to smoke at all; day two is also a success, but then on day three something goes wrong at work which causes stress, and the desire to smoke to counter the stress becomes overwhelming. Ah, they say, I'll just have one cigarette as I'm having a bad day. Next thing you know, it's day five and they are smoking again.

What happened? They were motivated but they failed to persist in the face of adversity. As soon as a challenge occurred, they used an excuse to give up. They lost sight of the bigger picture to focus on what was happening then. Neenan and Dryden (see Resources for their book on life coaching) explain that motivation consists of three components:

- Direction – what you are trying to do or achieve
- Effort – how hard you are trying
- Persistence – how long you continue trying.

We could say that to date, most of our efforts have gone into defining the direction. We now need to transfer our effort to the actual "doing" and ensure that we persist.

# Why do people give up?

But what causes us to give up? In a nutshell, it's mostly all the "emotional" obstacles we have identified on our challenges log: limiting beliefs, fears, unmet needs, etc. - things that are not easy to change and require us to take risks and work hard.

Neenan and Dryden give many reasons for failing to persist. I suggest you look at them all, and if you find that one is missing from your challenges log, you add it in.

- Focusing on instant gratification rather than the long-term goals (as in the stop smoking example).
- Spending all your time on the cause of a problem rather than figuring out a solution, e.g. telling yourself that if you only knew how it started, you could solve it.

- Believing that you are not good enough to face the challenge; issues of self-worth and self-confidence.

- Feeling that the change will cause you to become someone else or your life to become too different, e.g. you have been overweight all your life and the thought of being slim and attractive is scary.

- Wanting other people to help you and take responsibility for addressing your challenges, e.g. believing that someone else must change for you to have what you want.

- Thinking that you were born a certain way and therefore can't change, e.g. thinking that you don't have the right skills and stopping at that rather than thinking of ways to develop the skills.

- Fearing failure or success.

- Justifying giving up through lack of progress, whilst really the lack of progress is due to not confronting an issue.

- Thinking that you can't move from something or somewhere because you have invested too much to date. For example, you could have invested a lot in an approach that doesn't work and be reluctant to change your approach.

- Convincing yourself that you're too old, too young, too this, that or the other.

- Jumping from task to task, e.g. having given one public talk and thinking that all the clients should come from that single effort.

- Hidden agendas: saying that you are working on something when you are not.

- Believing that if you keep doing something change will occur even if you don't address the issues.

- Giving up because change is not occurring fast enough.

- Having vested interests in keeping the situation as it is. For example, complaining that your vision is not becoming real although you are working really hard could mean that you are getting the people around you to feel sorry for you and give you lots of attention.

- Being aware of the issue but using this as a reason not to do anything about it.

- Insufficient repletion, e.g. giving up before the new way of thinking has bedded in.

It's a long list but I'm hoping that reading it will have triggered some interesting thoughts on the excuses you use to give up.

# Daily work

It is the small regular steps you take that will help you get what you want in life. The things you do and say on a daily basis. Of course, some tasks on your plan will have dates, for example "book my typing course" or "sign up at the new gym". However, many of the actions we've discussed, particularly the ones that deal with changing behaviours or increasing your level of self-care, require daily efforts. Your thoughts are always with you and you eat and sleep every day. What we're hoping for is that eventually what you want to change will become habitual.

Unfortunately, developing new habits can take some time, depending on what you are trying to change and your personality. I'm hoping that the steps, the tools and the resources will help you make a quick shift, but realistically, all it may boil down to is daily effort and focus.

It is this need for regular and sustained effort that can cause us to give up. I said earlier in the book that, unfortunately, I can't just give you the instruction to change for it to happen. It's an emotional experience. To change, you have to think differently and view life from a different perspective. In addition, the change is often not one big thing but a series of little things.

What I want to encourage you to do in this step is to realise that persistence is key, figure out what causes you to give up and see what actions you could take daily to keep going. This is another good use for your diary. You can add tasks to your plan but you can also write in your diary what daily commitments you are making and use it to review how you're doing before you go to sleep (and as you write down all the good stuff that happened that day). We have two key tools to map our journey: our plan to keep track of our tasks (typically big tasks with dates) and our diary for actions that are smaller and need to be repeated. For example, we've used our diary for making appointments and we've mentioned using it to book "look after YOU" type activities. I'm now suggesting you use your diary to track other daily actions you want to take as well as your daily achievements.

Remember that in all this we are not aiming for perfection. One single new habit may be all you need to stay motivated and keep going. Be nice to yourself; don't think you'll get everything right first time. I've been interested in personal development for a long time and changing some of my behaviours still requires daily focus. What I can say, though, is that I have managed to change in many areas, and that realisation really keeps me going.

# Make it fly

Now let's put some of the techniques into action.

---

## STEP 20

## DAILY WORK

1. Pull out your plan and your challenges log.

2. Review your list of challenges and compare it to Neenan and Dryden's list. Is there anything in there that will cause you to give up and is not already on your log?

3. Think of some daily activities that could help you address your limiting beliefs and fears, increase your self-confidence and persist. Enter them in your diary. For example, write your affirmations in your diary and read them each morning.

4. Start carrying your diary with you and recording your thoughts. (There are some nice electronic diaries you can have on your phone!)

5. If you are already doing a good job of daily work, congratulate yourself and see if there are any opportunities to do even better. How well are you doing at looking after YOU? Book daily work activities in your personal diary.

---

# DO IT!

1. Get hold of your plan and review the tasks you have progressed according to what you set out to do in the last step. If you have completed some tasks, change their status to complete. If some have slipped, ask yourself why, commit to do something different and adjust your plan.

2. If a week has passed since you last updated your progress report, update it.

3. Build some time in your week to complete next week's tasks.

4. Extract the key issues and risks and how you will look to address them.

5. Add some decisions you have to make this week and a comment to encourage you to move forward. To help, you could pretend that you are reporting to someone else on your progress, or you could start reporting to a friend or to your life partner.

6. Build some time each morning and/or evening to sit in silence and visualise what you want (see the exercise in Step 3). Add this to your daily work.

# Step 21

## Remove barriers to success

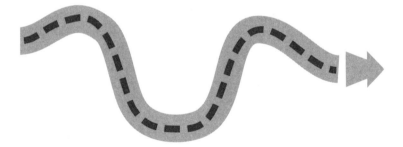

*"The world is wide, and I will not waste my life in friction when it could be turned into momentum."*

Frances E. Willard

In this step, we will look at how you can keep momentum high and "friction" low by finding clever ways to remove resistance and reduce stress rather than to push harder against obstacles. Deadlocks are created when two opposing forces push against each other with equal strength, for example your desire to move ahead and the stress caused by a fear. If the two are equal, things are likely to stop moving. To get them moving again, it's better to remove the block than to push harder and create more stress. In some cases, facing the fear may remove it, but in other cases you may need to find another way to prevent too much stress being created.

# Force, energy and friction

Every time you move something, you need to use force. We can therefore deduce that to move towards what you want, you will need to use "force" as well; we call this "taking action". Many of the steps and exercises have focused on encouraging you to take action.

To be able to apply "force", you need energy. If you have no energy, you will struggle to even move your pen. The aim of the "looking after YOU" section of the book was to ensure you were high in energy in your mind and body. This is physical energy and mental energy such as motivation.

Friction is what happens when motion (or in this case your actions) hits some resistance. Friction is the enemy of motion; it slows things down. If friction is strong enough, it will stop action dead in its track. Your challenges log is what you use to identify "friction" and decide what you'll do to remove it or lessen its impact.

# Creating momentum

Momentum is a force that makes it hard to stop moving ahead. The more momentum you have, the quicker things will start to happen and you'll get what you want. This is why big leaps forward often occur although you have not increased the force and the action. What you want behind your project is great momentum so that you can get big results without spending more energy. As I'm sure you're starting to realise, I believe that momentum is created by taking action regularly (small action typically) whilst at the same time consistently working to remove barriers. It's as if the impact of all the little actions adds up into something bigger because you've cleared the way.

# Pushing harder creates stress

We've discussed at length in the other steps the type of issues you may come across. What we've not really looked at is that when coming across some friction or resistance, it's best to try to remove what is causing it rather than to push harder. This is because pushing harder creates stress, and stress depletes your energy (and you need to save your energy to take action!). In this step, I'd like you to consider your challenges log from this new angle and to think how you can actually "remove" the barriers to success where possible rather than push harder, so that you can protect your energy and create momentum. Let's face it, if someone is resisting something, pushing harder is likely only to get them to dig their heels in. I'm sure the same is true about you.

# Reducing resistance by increasing your motivation

You can reduce resistance and remove obstacles by reinforcing the forces in your life that propel you forward, for example your motivation and desires for something different or your positive beliefs about yourself and your life. As a result, this will often reduce how resistant you are to something. We did a little bit on this when we logged some entries into your opportunity log.

Let's say that energy to take action comes from your desire for your life to change for the better; you've been feeling bad physically in recent months and you've had enough. We've looked at visualisation as a way to stay motivated and keep moving forward. Another way to do this could be to play on your aspiration to get out of a certain situation and reinforce it. For example, you could reduce your desire to smoke by increasing your disgust of it.

I stopped smoking more than 17 years ago. It wasn't the first time I'd tried to stop. In fact I had stopped several times before but always started again a few months later. The time I gave up for good, I had managed to last without a single cigarette for nearly a full year, having stopped as a New Year resolution at the beginning of 1994. On the night the behaviour was set for good, I was at the office Christmas party when a colleague offered me a cigarette. My resolve not to smoke was overcome by the party mood and probably a slight desire to "fit in" with the smoking crowd. So I took the cigarette, but because I hadn't smoked for so long, the first draw of smoke made me feel very sick. After that incident, and I must admit this wasn't planned, cigarettes became associated with feeling sick. It's now 2013 and I have not touched a cigarette since that night. I have zero desire to ever smoke again.

# Reducing resistance by removing the root cause

You could also remove resistance by addressing the root cause. This seems logical but sometimes the root cause is not obvious. Let's illustrate with the example of someone who is looking to become an actor, but whose inner voice constantly repeats "I'm not good enough to become an actor, why put myself through all this, best stay in my existing job and not suffer failure and rejection." We may be tempted to think that the issue is fear and encourage our actor friend to face the fear. However, for them, this may feel like pushing harder and create too much stress, stopping them from moving ahead.

Through some additional probing, we may find that the root cause is actually a lack of training rather than an issue of self-confidence. By registering for some drama classes, our actor will get the skills and practice they need, and as a result an increase in confidence. This feels a lot less stressful to them and they are very happy to move ahead.

# How about external resistance?

In both our examples, we've looked at resistance that came from inside ourselves (fears and beliefs). Resistance may also come from other people. In Step 9, you identified your success partners and qualified their attitude in relation to you getting what you want. When other people are resistant, use the same approach and look to find and remove the root cause. This is more likely to succeed than trying to coerce them into supporting you and your plans.

For example, if you find that your life partner is resistant to your change of career because they are worried about your joint income going down during the transition, building up a reserve in the bank to address their concern has a much better chance of success than saying to them "Why can't you trust me? It'll be all right."

# Make it fly

It is now time to use your imagination and look for clever ways to address challenges by reducing resistance rather than by pushing harder against the block.

---

### STEP 21 EXERCISE

### REMOVING RESISTANCE

1. Get hold of your challenges log and your list of success partners.
2. Review how you are planning to address the challenge and brainstorm whether there would be clever ways to reduce resistance.
3. Review your plan to take out the actions where you were pushing harder and replace them with ways to remove resistance.

---

## DO IT!

1. Get hold of your plan and commit to moving some of the tasks forward in the next week.
2. If you've amended your plan, amend your progress report to mirror the changes.
3. Build some time in your week to complete next week's tasks.
4. Extract the key challenges and how you will look to address them.
5. Add some decisions you have to make this week and a comment to encourage you to move forward. To help, you could

pretend that you are reporting to someone else on your progress, or you could start reporting to a friend or to your life partner.

6. Build some time each morning and/or evening to sit in silence and visualise what you want (see the exercise in Step 3). Add this to your daily work.

7. Make sure you keep your energy up by having some 'looking after YOU' type tasks in your diary.

# Step 22

# The importance of alignment

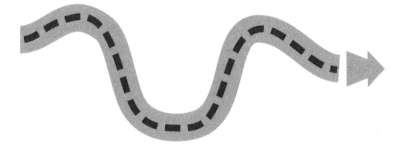

*"If people aren't in sync, things won't work out well."*
Stephen Hopkins

In the previous step, we talked about momentum. Another way to create momentum is to ensure that all the bits needed for your vision to become real are in alignment, that there isn't a bit under the surface blocking the flow. When everything around you aligns to push you in the direction of what you want, momentum and flow are created and one step you take seems to have the impact of 10 similar steps in a situation where nothing aligns.

There are three areas to look at when working to create alignment: yourself, other people and the structures around you. In this step, we will look at each of these areas in the context of the work you have achieved to date to allow you to get an overall sense of how much alignment and momentum you have and in which areas you need to invest more effort.

# Yourself

You are the key to achieving your vision and we have spent some time identifying how your values align to what you want, which of your fears and beliefs will get in the way and whether you have all that you need to make things happen. We have also looked at minimising distractions, increasing your self-confidence and taking responsibility. If you have followed the exercises, your findings in these areas have been incorporated in your challenges log and in your plan to ensure that all issues are worked through, all risks mitigated and all areas of lack and need addressed.

For example, if you have discovered that you lack some of the skills you need, your plan will have an action for you to attend some courses and you should now be well on your way to acquiring the necessary skills. What I'd like you to think about now is whether you have truly put the effort in to address each of the issues you've uncovered or whether you've focused on the easy areas and have neglected the hard ones. For example, you may have gone on a course but not done much about addressing a fear in another area. The outcome of this would be that you'll be gaining great skills but may be ignoring the one thing that will create the most momentum. Also, your fears will be blocking the flow.

# Other people

We've looked at identifying your success partners and at the work that was needed to ensure they were all on your side. How well have you done at getting them all on your side and fully supportive? Since the project to get what you want may be a lonely pursuit, having positive people to discuss challenges and celebrate successes is key. As I write this, a friend of mine has just opened a new foodstore and his girlfriend has posted pictures of his new shop and himself at work on Facebook. What a great idea! Not only is he getting her support but also other friends, like us, are now posting messages of encouragement. This must be creating brilliant momentum for him (plus, I guess, it's generating great publicity!).

If you are not getting enough encouragement from the people around you, go back to the Step 9 exercise and look to develop it further. If some people are encouraging, why don't you discuss this issue with them?

# The structures around you

You want to improve your health, so you have joined the gym, you go to bed to get a good night's sleep and you've changed your diet. However, there are "structures" in your life which keep getting in the way. For example, your work schedule is so heavy that you end up working many more hours than you should and you are often too tired to make your gym appointment. Or, maybe, the way you keep in touch with your friends is by joining them down the pub on the Friday night where you end up drinking too much and not sleeping well. Your habits or commitments are not aligned to your vision.

What can you do? Although this will seem dramatic, if you are truly committed to reaching your goals, you will need to do something about aligning your habits, lifestyle and commitment. "But I can hardly leave my job", I hear you say. My reply is "Why not?". If being healthy is your vision and you work in an organisation that does not support a good work–life balance then this will always stand in the way of achieving what you want. The lack of alignment between your organisation's values and your own needs to be addressed. And, yes, it may have to come to you finding another job.

However, what you could do first is test your assumption: maybe you are the one who created the perception that you loved working all hours because you used to be that way. Now that you have decided to change, it would be worth testing with your boss what their views are. You may actually find that they are willing to support what you want; maybe they are going through a similar change themselves. It's not uncommon to find that when you are looking to change something in yourself and your life, strangely you start attracting people with similar wishes. If, however, you find that your boss and your organisation have values very different from your own and no desire to support your vision, then it may be time to call it a day.

In the above example, leisure and work were out of alignment, but there are other structures in your life to consider. How about your love life? Does it align with your vision? If you are looking to feel great but your relationships aren't working, I'd say that there is some need for alignment. Here's a list of areas to consider: leisure, physical environment, business/career, finances, health, family and friends, love/romance and personal growth.

# Make it fly

I suspect that if you have done the work on values and success partners, these areas will be well catered for. What we have missed and what you may wish to focus on here is aligning the structures in your life: work, family, leisure, spirituality, love, etc.

---

**STEP 22 EXERCISE**

**ALIGNMENT**

1. Look at whether each area of your life aligns with your vision. If it doesn't, add the issue to your challenges log and brainstorm a solution.

2. Thinking of the three areas of alignment together (yourself, other people, structures), consider whether you have been working equally in all of them, whether you are avoiding some issues and what you could do to create more alignment and momentum.

---

3. If you find some new issues, enter them in your challenges log. If you find new actions you could take, enter them on your plan. If the issue or action is already there, commit to doing something about it in the next seven days.

## DO IT!

1. Get hold of your plan and commit to moving some of the new tasks forward in the next week. Enter this in your progress report for this week.

2. Build some time in your week to complete next week's tasks.

3. Extract the key issues and risks and how you will look to address them. Update your progress report.

4. Add some decisions you have to make this week to your progress report and a comment to encourage you to move forward.

5. Build some time each morning and/or evening to sit in silence and visualise what you want (see the exercise in Step 3). Add this to your daily work.

6. Ensure there are some "looking after YOU" tasks booked in your diary.

# Step 23

## Develop a support system

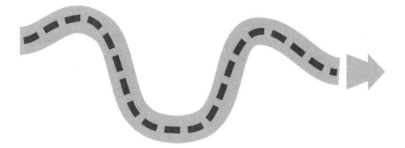

*"Tell everyone what you want to do and someone will want to help you do it."*

W. Clement Stone

What if your success partners are well meaning but not that helpful? For example, if what you want is to write a book, they may not always be the best judge of whether what you have written is any good. Not wanting to upset your feelings or simply not being that well trained in what makes good and bad writing, they may be a little too quick to compliment your work. In this step, we will look at other forms of support.

*"When life gets tough, don't be ashamed or too proud to ask for help."*

*Author unknown*

Don't go thinking your success partners are not important – they are, particularly if they were less than convinced about your project when you first started and you've now managed to get them on side. Do what you can to keep them there. Having your loved ones oppose your goals is really not somewhere you want to be, particularly since you'll have enough challenges along the way. In this step, we will look at ways to supplement the support you already get from your success partners. This may take the form of getting unbiased or specialised advice or being kept accountable and challenged.

The list below doesn't claim to be comprehensive but it should help you get a good idea of (a) whether support would be beneficial, (b) the types you naturally prefer, and (c) whether you should go ahead and get the help. I have listed the support types in this order: something you can do on your own, working with a group or individual support. The aim is to explain what is available so that you can make an educated decision about what you need and invest in what is right for you. It is important to note that this may also change during the journey; for example, you may need individual support to get started, then swap for group support once you feel you are well on your way.

By now, I hope you will have made good use of the book, followed up on the recommended resources and accessed the website to get even more support and information. If this is working well for you, carry on! Also, do remember to use the book as a "tool". Go back on steps when you need to, rework an exercise or reread a chapter for inspiration. If you feel you need more, below are some things you may wish to investigate further.

# Training courses and workshops

Through the companion website, you will be able to find out about training courses and workshops. This is a good way to go into the method and the steps in more depth but also to get feedback on the work you're doing.

If you like to work in a group, training and workshops may be right for you. Through training, you will be able to get access to live advice on the steps, and through the workshops you will be able to get some support with the exercises. The disadvantage is that the advice and support will be less extensive than with coaching and mentoring where the coach or the mentor is fully dedicated to you. The trainer or workshop facilitator will have a group to look after, so even if the group is small, their time will be limited. A definite advantage, though, is that you will get a bunch of people to brainstorm with when you hit an issue and to encourage you along the way. There's nothing like sharing with people on a similar path.

So if you like to work in a group, signing up for training sessions or a workshop may be what you need.

# Mentoring

Mentoring is where someone with expertise in your area of interest works with you and offers the benefits of their experience. For example, if what you want is to open a garden centre, your mentor would be someone who has done just that: successfully set up and run a garden centre. So if domain-specific advice would be beneficial to you then a mentor may be something you look for.

Something to consider when hiring a mentor is whether they have formal mentoring or coaching skills. If you find a mentor who knows your specialism and is also able to coach you on limitations, this can be a very powerful combination.

Another consideration is that your mentor may or may not be trained in the method themselves, so you may need a combination of types of support, for example the book and the companion website for the actual method but also a mentor for the expert advice on your project.

A mentor will, however, be great to challenge your limitations as they are the living proof that success is possible. Finding a mentor who has done what you want to do may be just what you need at some points in your journey. And again, you could combine having a mentor with other means of support, or you could talk to a mentor just a few times to get information or an opportunity to brainstorm.

# Specialised coaching (using the method and other tools, so not just basic coaching)

If what you need is to be shown how to use the method, kept accountable, challenged and provided with a safe space to address issues and develop your ideas, then coaching may be what you need. Although coaching has grown in popularity, the process is still misunderstood. A good coach is not someone who has experience in your area of choice. In fact, it is best if they don't. A coach is someone who will use the tools and techniques of coaching with the method to help you move forward with your project but will make sure that the element of the journey that is "you" is fully addressed. They will make sure that you don't stand in the way of your vision. They are a brilliant resource for limitations, beliefs, fears and so on, and for accountability.

You can get access to coaching programmes through the companion website or you can choose to work with an independent coach.

# Make it fly

If you start to struggle, don't make the mistake of giving up on your vision because you thought you should do it alone. Remember that the goal is to get what you want, not to demonstrate that you can be self-sufficient.

---

## STEP 23 EXERCISE
## DEVELOP A SUPPORT SYSTEM

1. Think of the area in which you need the most support: understanding and applying the method? Keeping yourself accountable? Helping you address personal limitations? Expert advice in a

---

particular area? Someone to challenge you and help you get out of your comfort zone?

2. Think of your preferred form of support: do you prefer to work on your own? Do you get energised from being part of a group? Would you benefit more from one-to-one support?

3. Consider how much time and money you can invest in support: is attending a regular training/workshop session possible? Would you rather set the time you attend training and maybe combine it with coaching? Do you need a mentor or could you buy a book on how to set up a successful photography business? Do you have a limited budget available for this for now, or do you think investing would actually mean that you get there faster? Is there something you could give up to release some money (e.g. smoking!)?

4. List your answers and then choose the ideal type of support for you. Go ahead and identify where your best support will come from.

5. This week, commit to booking the course/session, meeting up with a mentor for coffee, buying a book listed in the Resources, or joining the community on the companion website.

## DO IT!

1. Get hold of your plan and commit to moving some of the new tasks forward in the next week. Enter this in your progress report for this week.

2. Build some time in your week to complete next week's tasks.

3. Extract the key issues and risks and how you will look to address them. Update your progress report.

4. Add some decisions you have to make this week to your progress report and a comment to encourage you to move forward.

5. Build some time each morning and/or evening to sit in silence and visualise what you want (see the exercise in Step 3). Add this to your daily work.

6. Look after YOU!

# WHAT IF THINGS GO WRONG?

*"Do not turn back when you are just at the goal."*

Publilius Syrus

What if you are taking the steps but getting no or very limited results? Or what if you are not having fun moving your vision forward any more? We discussed this briefly in Step 16; however, I would like to spend a little bit more time on this topic, because we need to make sure that if you are about to make a major decision about your goals, you make it from a position of strength rather than from one of frustration or fear. Let's look at a few situations to illustrate what could be happening.

## I keep trying but nothing works

You have a plan with a list of clear actions, you've moved forward with lots of tasks but you're not seeing the expected results. Your motivation is low and you feel like giving up. The following thoughts are starting to come into your head: "Why am I bothering with this? I was fine before. Maybe I'm just not meant to have what I want." STOP. Now forget all that has happened, relax and spend 10 minutes doing your visualisation exercise. Do you still get motivated and energised? If you could have what you want tomorrow without any effort, would you still want it? If the answer is yes then you need to take an honest look at whether you are going about it the right way. Maybe it's your approach that is wrong? Maybe the actions you are taking are just not the right ones? Maybe you're taking all the "safe" actions and no risk at all? A good way to make sure is to find someone who already has what you are after and talk to them. How did they achieve it? Was it hard? How long did it take? What were the key things that got them there? How much effort did they have to put in to see some results?

# Are you lying to yourself?

So, when you say you've "tried everything", how many things did you really try? How long have you been actively working on your project? Have you really completed all the exercises fully? Have you neglected some key areas, convincing yourself that they weren't important (because you were scared or even a tad lazy)? If you've tried three things and you've been working actively on your project for only two weeks, I would say that you have not put in enough effort.

The difficulty when working on your vision on your own is that it's easy to convince yourself that you're doing everything right. You may know that you aren't, and choose to ignore the issue, or simply you may not be seeing the problem. You may need to get some help or to think outside the box. Talk to your success partners: what do they think? Would they say that you have tried enough? Better still, get some independent advice: as I said earlier, find someone who has been there before, or post a question on an online forum, or better still, find a support group or hire a coach. There's nothing like sharing your story with a bunch of positive people to get energised again, to get confirmation that you're going about it the right way or to get some ideas how you could do things differently.

# I'm not sure what I want is right for me

What if you did the visualisation exercise and didn't feel motivated about your project any more? Before you decide to give up, I would like you to ask yourself why you wanted this thing in the first place - what was the experience you were you trying to create? Could it be that you got what you wanted another way and your project is now less important? Let's say what you wanted was to increase your status in the community, and to do so you were looking to move to a bigger house. For some reason, you don't seem to find the right house. At the same time, you get a promotion at work, which substantially increases your status in the organisation. Your need for recognition is now satisfied and it may be that the house thing is not so important any more; you'd rather focus your energy on your career. In that case, I would say that you did get the experience you wanted to create but via a different mechanism. Ask yourself whether your promotion is now giving you what you wanted. It may be that you decide that, for now, you will park the idea of moving home because, although you'd still like to do that some day, you're really excited about your new job.

# Accept that some things are just hard

I would love to be able to say to you that making it as a writer, actor or musician, losing weight, improving your health and lifestyle and returning to work after your kids have grown up are easy to do if you do everything I'm suggesting, but I can't. What I'm promising is that if you follow the steps and you persist, you will get what you want. However, I cannot guarantee that it will be easy. In fact, I can pretty much guarantee the opposite. If you have found someone who has been there, ask them how long it took and the amount of effort they had to put in. For every successful writer, actor and musician, there are several people who didn't make it. The difference is persistence. They kept at it even when things looked like they weren't moving, or when something didn't work they just tried something else. They kept at it even if they couldn't see the whole staircase. Knowing this may be all you need to keep going.

Remember that a significant number of people *do* make it, and often these people are not necessarily the best; they may be just good enough and seriously determined. Look around for some examples of success. It may be just a matter of you realising and accepting that you will need to put in some serious effort. Look after yourself, build your energy and just put in the effort! Come on! What is the alternative?

# Do you have what you need?

Do you have all the resources you need to get to your vision? If you want to be a musician, are your skills good enough to succeed in a highly

WHAT IF THINGS GO WRONG?

competitive industry? I did say that you don't always have to be the best but you do have to be good enough or interesting enough. Would you benefit from taking more lessons? Would you benefit from giving some free concerts in your local pub and getting some practice? If what you want is to lose weight, do you actually know what makes up a good diet? Could you do with visiting a dietician and getting a menu designed just for you? A menu that you would find appealing rather than one from a book. If you want to go back to work but your skills are rusty, could you do with some refresher courses?

Years ago, I wanted to move up the ladder at work. I felt I had picked up enough skills along the way but I didn't have the right qualifications, so my CV kept being turned down. To succeed, I had to go back to university and study for a postgraduate diploma. In this case what mattered was that I could demonstrate via my education that I was qualified. I may have felt I had the skills, but this was an area of work where a formal qualification carried some weight, whether I liked it or not. Maybe I would have ended up progressing without my studies eventually, but, to be honest, the diploma also gave me some additional confidence and a chance to lecture, so in the end it was hard work but it was absolutely the right thing to do for me.

# Make it fly

If you are experiencing a need to adjust your vision, complete the exercise below. If you are still happy and motivated about your goals and things are going great, then please just move on to the next step. And remember, it is not wrong to re-evaluate and change what you want or the approach.

## REWRITE WHAT YOU WANT

1. Get hold of all the materials you have produced to date. If you have filed the materials under each step on a computer, create a new folder and copy every file to that one folder so that all your material is in one place.

2. If you have more than one version of your plan and challenges log, only copy the latest version.

3. Review everything and make written notes on what comes to mind as you read or adjust your material accordingly. How else could you go about this? Did you brainstorm more than one approach; could you try one of the alternatives? How much effort have you really put in? Are you playing safe? Do you need to up your game?

4. Find someone who has succeeded at what you are trying to do and go talk to them.

# CONCLUSION: WHERE TO NOW?

*"The most effective way to do it, is to do it."*

*Amelia Earhart*

Congratulations on reaching the end of the book. I hope that the techniques have helped you clarify what you want, plan it and make it happen (if not in whole, enough to prove to yourself that you can have what you want and to keep going). Also, that you have understood that a mechanical or an emotional approach alone is not enough, that you have to combine the two.

Hopefully the method will have also taught you how to stay on track and keep going, whether the journey is easy or you have to deal with obstacles. And if you found that keeping motivated was difficult on your own, you have either joined the online community or hired a coach. There is nothing like the support of other people to give you encouragement.

Hopefully, by working through the steps you will have also found tools and techniques that speak to you. I have tried, as much as I could, to present things from different angles so that if the first way didn't suit you, the second or the third might. I have tried my best to create "ah ha" moments for you and hopefully cause you to shift a limiting belief, change a behaviour or face a fear. When I work with people directly, I can use the techniques I sense will work best with them, but with a book I can't do that. So, if you have found that some steps overlapped, I did this on purpose because I wanted to help a wide range of people but also because, to be honest, when it comes to change it's good to have some repetition, as often, in order to change, people have to hear the same thing over and over again.

# Feedback, please

The method has been developed from my years of experience making change happen in organisations but also in my own life and the lives of others. I have been refining it for years and would love to continue, so if you have some feedback, good or bad, do write to me via the website and let me know what you think could be improved, as well as what you think has worked well for you. And if you have had some success with the method, make sure you let me know, as there is nothing like showcasing success to encourage other people to go for what they want in life! Your experiences could encourage someone to finally take the plunge.

# This isn't the end

Wherever you are on the journey to your vision, I hope you'll come back to the book often and will really use it as a tool. I hope that you will go back to the steps as you need to and will dip in often, to get what you want either this time or the next one. I hope your copy of the book will be full of notes, bent pages and even coffee stains (unless of course it's the electronic version, but you can still make notes on that).

I wrote this book to encourage you to go after what you want, because I believe that the more people who do, the happier our world will be. Keep wanting the best for yourself and keep going for it. Don't deny the world your skills, talents and light.

# RESOURCES

## Wellbeing

Grace, J.L. Look Great Naturally, Hay House, 2010 and
www.imperfectlynatural.com
Hay, L. You Can Heal Your Life, Eden Grove Editions, 1984 and any other
book by Louise Hay
Headspace. www.getsomeheadspace.com
Holford, P. The Optimum Nutrition Bible, Piatkus, 2004
Marber, I. The Food Doctor Ultimate Diet, Dorling Kindersley, 2009
Parking, J.C. f**k it, Hay House, 2007
Whiteman, J. 9 Days to Feel Fantastic, Hay House, 2012

## Behaviours

Covey, S. The 7 Habits of Highly Effective People, Simon & Schuster, 2004
Ford, D. The Dark Side of the Light Chasers, Hodder Paperbacks, 2001
Jeffers, S. Feel the Fear and Do It Anyway, Arrow, 1993
Laurence, T. The Hoffman Process, Bantam, 2004
Neenan, M. and Dryden, W. Life Coaching: A Cognitive-Behavioural Ap-
proach, Routledge, 2002
Yeung, R. Confidence, Prentice Hall Life, 2008

## Money

Carlyle, M.C. Money Magnet Mindset, Hay House, 2012

## *Positive psychology*

Haidt, J. The Happiness Hypothesis, William Heinemann, 2006

Seligman, M. Authentic Happiness, Nicholas Brealey, 2003

# INDEX